Modern Collector's Dolls

Seventh Series

Patricia R. Smith

COLLECTOR BOOKS

A Division of Schroeder Publishing Co., Inc.

The current values in this book should be used only as a guide. They are not intended to set prices, which vary from one section of the country to another. Auction prices as well as dealer prices vary greatly and are affected by condition as well as demand. Neither the Author nor the Publisher assumes responsibility for any losses that might be incurred as a result of consulting this guide.

Searching For A Publisher?

We are always looking for knowledgeable people considered to be experts within their fields. If you feel that there is a real need for a book on your collectible subject and have a large comprehensive collection, contact Collector Books.

Book layout and cover design by Karen Geary

Additional copies of this book may be ordered from:
Collector Books
P.O. Box 3009
Paducah, Kentucky 42002-3009

@$24.95. Add $2.00 for postage and handling.

Copyright: Patricia R. Smith, 1995

Printed by IMAGE GRAPHICS, INC., Paducah, Kentucky

Dedication

This dedication is to Genie Jenright who loved dolls, life, family, and friends. Everyone who knew her loved her back. She was special and will be remembered. We dedicate this book to all the special people who loved dolls and are now gone. They are missed by everyone who knew them.

Credits

Hazel Adams, Marian Alessi, Gloria Anderson, Chaye "Sara" Arotsky, Betty Barcliff, Sandy Johnson-Barts, Sally Bethschieder, Kay Bransky, Renie Culp, Sandra Cummins, Ellen Dodge, Doll Cradle (8719 W. 50th Terr., Merriam, KS 66203), Marie Ernst, Frasher Doll Auctions (Rt. 1, Box 72, Oak Grove, MO 64075), Maureen Fukushima, Idona Furnish, Pat Graff, Karen Geary, Susan Giradot, Jacqueline Halcomb, Sharon Hamilton, Marcia Jarmush, Genie Jinright, Chris Johnson, Phyllis Houston-Kates, Jo Keelen, Mildred Lasky, Theo Lindley, Kris Lundquist, Margaret Mandel, Shirley and Amy Merrill, Ellyn McCorkell, Sharon McDowell, Chris McWilliams, Peggy Millhouse, Jay Minter, Jeannie Mauldin, Jeannie Nespoli, Mary Paine, Peggy Pergande, June Schultz, Charmaine Shields, Shirley's Doll House (P.O. Box 99, Wheeling, IL 60090), Virginia Sofie, Pat Sparks, Sheila Stephenson, Karen Stephenson, Helena Street, David Spurgeon, Martha Sweeny, Charleen Thanos, Turn of the Century Antiques (1475 S. Broadway, Denver, CO 80210), Carol Turpen, Kathy Tvrdik, Jeannie Venner, Mike Way, Ann Wencel, Marie Wolfe, Patricia A. Wood, Glorya Woods.

Cover Photo Credit

MISS CURITY by Ideal. 21" - $450.00. *Courtesy Peggy Millhouse*

Note

In this book, there may be dolls that have been previously shown in the *Doll Values* series. There could be dolls that have appeared in the *Modern Collector's Dolls* series, but they will be pictured in different outfits or in costumes that need to be seen in color to be appreciated. Prices are based on near mint, clean, original dolls with the exception of Madame Alexander dolls whose prices reflect perfect, mint dolls.

Updated information for *Modern Collector's Dolls Series 1–5* is listed in the appendix beginning on page 276.

Contents

☙ Preface ☙

The second most-often asked question of me is "How did you get started writing about dolls?" What is the first question, you ask? "What is the value?"

Once upon a time, there was a professional, Dr. Patricia R. Smith, Ph.D., who worked in the humanities with socially dysfunctional families. One very hot, muggy summer day, my favorite aunt visited from our hometown of Santa Barbara, CA. She said she collected dolls and asked if I would watch out for them for her, especially one called Barbie. As I nodded "yes," my thoughts were "the breakdown came from living so long in a place called Barbara." She went to visit elsewhere for a couple of weeks and left me to my wondering.

I finally managed the time to go to the library and found some books on dolls, one even had modern dolls. I came, I looked, and I set out to conquer the world of dolls, spurred on by my thoughts of a big hug and a bigger smile from that favorite aunt.

I went to the Goodwill store — I was told things were cheap there. I purchased three large boxes of dolls for $4.35. My aunt returned. I felt I should leave her alone to go over my great discoveries. Before long, she reappeared — her face long, her arms at her sides. I was not going to get a hug, nor a smile. I waited. Then she told me she did not want dolls with their limbs gone, their eyes punched out, their hair cut to the scalp, nor Barbie dolls who had been abused with a felt- tip marker.

My smile and apology were weak, but I made it through lunch and seeing my *least* favorite aunt off on the next leg of her journey.

My ego was destroyed. As I disposed of the dolls into green lawn bags, I was determined to clear my name. I took time off from work and set about writing my own doll book. In two weeks in the fall of 1971, I bought 1,234 dolls for less than $400.00 total. I bought from thrift shops all over the city. Prices ranged from 5¢ to $7.50. (One doll was a S.F.B.J. Jumeau, all original. It was shown in my first *Modern Collector's Dolls* book.) Most were nude and dirty. I swore every doll would be clean and looking as good as I could make them. I washed them, combed their hair, and dressed them in clothing that I bought by the boxload. Dolls were *everywhere* — down the hall and in every room. What about my husband? He needed a hobby and soon became my "official photographer" with my mother's camera.

What do I mean by "original?" What is *that*? I had to do another book because I did not know about original dolls in the first book. During this time I also researched companies and workers, went on interviews, and learned most doll companies had a common denominator — they all had fires that wiped out their records. I grew in knowledge as the field of doll collecting expanded and overtook all other hobbies but stamp collecting. Now, 40 books later, I am still learning, still making mistakes, and still trying to make up for it!

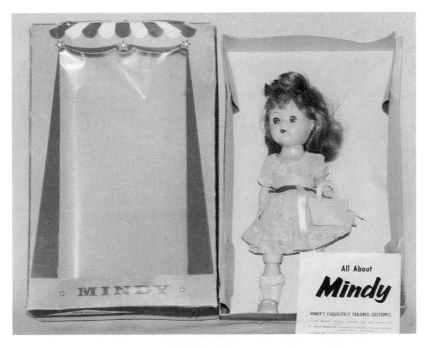

7½" MINDY made by Active Doll Corp. in late 1957. She is actually a GINGER purchased from Cosmopolitian by many companies that did not make their own dolls. She is all hard plastic and has jointed knees and large round eyes. $50.00. *Courtesy Maureen Fukushima.*

MINDY in her original trunk that has her name on the front. She is dressed in #19 "School Days." Her first year on the market was 1957. $95.00 up. *Courtesy Maureen Fukushima.*

MINDY is in her original trunk and dressed in #35 "Gypsy." She is a straight leg walker. $60.00. *Courtesy Maureen Fukushima*

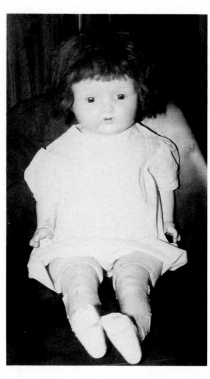

Fat-cheeked child with composition and cloth body. Has tin sleep eyes and molded teeth. Catalogs from 1928–1932 show her as ANETTE. Made by Acme Dolls, Chicago. Mint - $125.00; fair - $55.00. *Courtesy Betty Barcliff.*

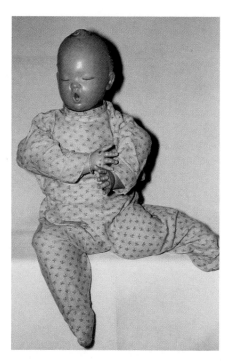

21" HANES BABY was used for advertsing newborn wear and sleepers in the early 1950s. Outfits came in various colors and prints. Vinyl head and arms with cloth body and legs. Has painted sleep eyes and wide open yawning mouth. Vinyl made during this time can turn color or become sticky. Mint - $150.00; with vinyl changes - $60.00. *Courtesy Kathy Tvrdik.*

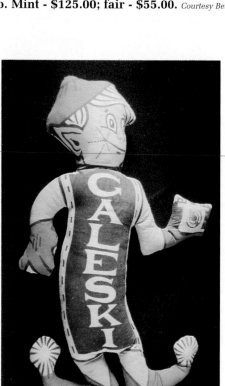

16½" stuffed advertising doll for Caleski. Doll was made for opticians who also sold and processed film. From the early 1950s. $45.00. *Courtesy Phyllis Houston-Kates.*

Three early 17" LITTLE MISS SUNBEAM dolls made for the Sunbeam Bread Company. The sitting doll with red lips is the first issue and was made of good quality plastic. The others are made of lightweight plastic with vinyl heads and arms. They have pink lips and longer eyelashes. All are marked "Eegee" on head. A variety of printed cloth was used for dresses. 1959–1965. Mint - $65.00; played with - $45.00. *Courtesy Marie Ernst.*

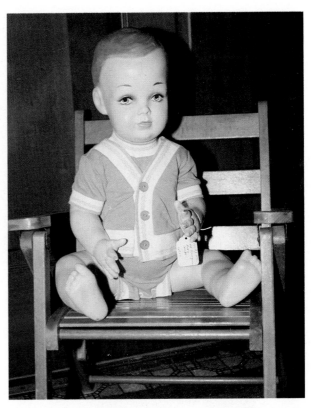

19" doll made of heavy papier maché with painted features. Springs in arms and neck allow doll to move side to side electronically. Chair marked "Ooo - Ooo! Is I Happy!! See what Mommy gives me!" and "The Geo. F. Jones Co. Greensburg, Pa." (Doll in chair - 39" overall.) Mint - $200.00. *Courtesy Sandra Cummins.*

22" mannequin with very pretty face from late 1930s through early 1950s. Has painted features and hair. $165.00. *Courtesy Jeannie Mauldin.*

Four BUSTER BROWN advertising dolls. Large boy and girl are 32" tall. The smaller boy and the sitting boy are 25". All have molded hair and painted eyes. Marked "Buster Brown, Old King Cole, Inc." Each - $165.00–225.00. *Courtesy Jeannie Mauldin.*

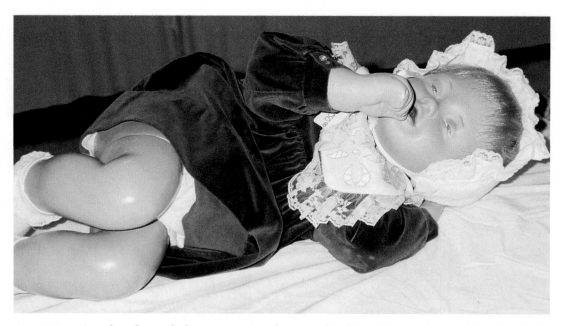

A mannequin of a sleepy baby. Has painted eyes, glued-on wig, and open/closed mouth. Circa 1960s. $185.00. *Courtesy Theo Lindley.*

28" MR. MAGOO with vinyl head and stuffed cloth body. Dressed in baseball uniform with removable felt cap. General Electric logo patch on uniform and cap. Left hand forms baseball glove. Baseball is in right hand. Marked on head "1967 UPA Pictures Inc." $185.00. *Courtesy Jeannie Mauldin.*

14" all cloth doll made for Gillette Razor Blades in 1974. $25.00. *Courtesy Gloria Anderson.*

All cloth CHICKEN OF THE SEA MERMAIDS. 14" in box was made by Mattel in 1974. 12" was made by Acone Premium in 1991. **Each - $50.00.** *Courtesy Jeannie Mauldin.*

20" ENERGIZER BUNNY tagged "Energizer 1989 Brand Batteries. Animal Fair. Trademark of Eveready Battery Co., Inc." **$55.00.** *Courtesy Jeannie Mauldin.*

Three advertising dolls made for Northern Bath Tissue. Cloth bodies with vinyl heads and limbs. All original. Doll on left is from 1986, center is from 1988, and right is from 1990. **Each - $35.00.** *Courtesy Jeannie Mauldin.*

⋐ A&H Doll Mfg. Corp. ⋑

The A&H Doll Mfg. Corp. and Dutchess Dolls made the majority of the popular priced 8" to 12" dolls often referred to as Dime Dolls. Most of these dolls have one-piece bodies and legs. They have sleep or painted eyes, glued-on mohair strand for wig, and stapled-on clothes. These two companies are also known for better quality dolls such as A&H's Dolls of Destiny from 1953. The 12 costumes represent famous ladies in history and were very well made. The dolls were 12" tall and the clothes are usually tagged.

In 1956, A&H made a 9" Ginny look-alike doll named Marcie. She was a walker with a saran wig. Down the entire sides of the doll, the molding seams are visible. She was boxed as a dressed doll or wearing just her panties, socks, and shoes. During the first year of the doll's production, there were 16 outfits that could be purchased separately. A&H put an 11½" Barbie copy on the market in 1962, also named Marcie. She even had a black and white striped bathing suit like Barbie doll's.

There was an 8" Marcie that was a pin-jointed hip walker and a regular walker with jointed knees. Another version used the same body as the jointed knee doll but had a vinyl head and rooted hair.

A&H's most popular and best known doll is the 8" Gigi. She had sleep eyes with molded lashes, a large navel, and good finger and toe detail. (There are no dimples above the fingers but two above the toes.) Her head turned as she walked. The side seams of the limbs are usually not flat and mold lines stand out.

A&H also made a 10½" Little Miss Revlon type doll, also named Gigi, that had sleep eyes, regular joints, movable waist, and high heels. She was unmarked and made from 1957 to 1959.

These 9" MARCIE DAILY DOLLY dolls originally were sold boxed, dressed only in panties, shoes, and socks. She is a walker with highly visible mold seams. Her sleep eyes had molded lids, and her saran wig came in various styles. Shown is a tosca blonde with pigtails and brunette with rolled hairdo. In 1956, she had 16 outfits which were sold separately. $50.00 each.

Courtesy Maureen Fukushima.

Typical boxed 8" GIGI made of all hard plastic with sleep eyes and molded lashes. Mold seams stand out. This doll is shown in an original outfit. Also shown is a majorette dress, the same outfit shown on the front of the brochure. GIGI had many outfits that were sold separately. $50.00 up.

Courtesy Peggy Millhouse.

Left: 7½" GIGI in her original plastic dome bell. It must be noted other companies used the dome showcase. If the paper sticker has been washed or scratched off, it is difficult to determine if a doll and dome have been paired correctly. Right: GIGI out of the dome. She is a walker doll with legs far apart. She is wearing an original nurse uniform but is missing shoes. Each - $50.00 up. *Courtesy Maureen Fukushima.*

12" KIT CARSON made by A.H.I. of Hong Kong. Vinyl and plastic with gripper hands. Sold through discount stores in 1971. $18.00. *Courtesy David Spurgeon.*

Alexander Doll Company

Doll collectors want to know what is happening in the doll world, especially with their favorite companies or artists. This is most often directed at the Madame Alexander doll company. Yes, there have been changes — some we like; some we do not. The times are changing and as doll collectors, we must move with the pace of the doll world or find ourselves lost.

In the past, we have always thought of the Madame Alexander organization in terms of one woman, one firm, and one president (Mr. Bill Birnbaum). Yet the company has grown through the years and is now known as the Alexander Doll Company, parent to many toy firms. (See graph below for the Alexander corporate structure.)

Most of what we hear about the Madame Alexander dolls is good. People love them. The only negative we have seen or heard is about the hair fiber in recent years. If the hair is played with or exposed to humidity, it becomes oily and straightens. No matter how long it is left in curlers, it remains straight. (A few years ago, Horsman dolls had the same problem.)

Another hair concern is the lack of styling on recent dolls, except for the 8" models.

We do know that the older dolls are selling, and any that are exceptional are exceeding the price guides. The new dolls sell well each year. The older medium quality dolls are hardly selling at all. Do not pass up these dolls! If the face color is good and the hair is fixable, you might have a great buy, especially if you can find an original dress for it.

For more information about Madame Alexander dolls, Collector Books offers several doll titles, including *Madame Alexander Collector's Dolls*, *The World of Alexanderkins*, *The Collector's Encyclopedia of Madame Alexander Dolls*, and the annual *Madame Alexander Collector's Dolls Price Guide*.

Collecting Madame Alexander dolls is fun. The search for the perfect example can be a pain in the neck and can put a hole in a budget, but it is worth it when we finally do spot *our* doll. The newer, even this year's dolls, are fun to mull over and decide which ones you cannot live without. No question about it — Madame Alexander dolls are here to stay!

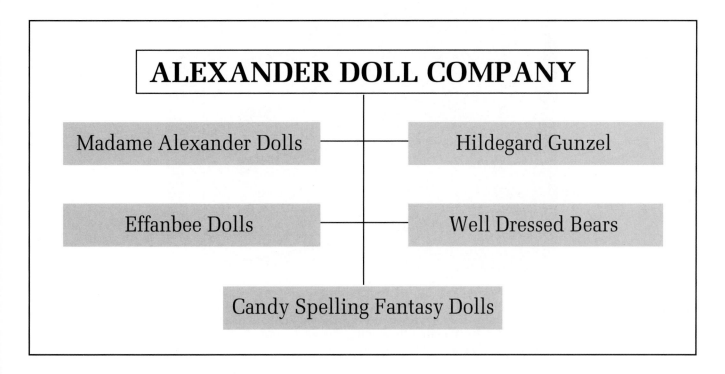

7½" set of DIONNE QUINTS dressed in original clothes and bibs. Basket is new. (Note: The quints have their own colors. Yvonne - pink, Annette - yellow, Cecile - green, Emilie - lavender, and Marie - blue. This was the only way Dr. Defoe and nurses could tell which baby girl they were attending.) Set - $1,200.00. *Courtesy Virginia Sofie.*

Rare wooden bath set for the DIONNE QUINTS. It is both a shower and a bath and has their names across the top. There are shelves on either side for their towels and washcloths. Scale is to an 8" doll. Marked "Scully Wooden Toys Mfg. Co. of Canada." Shown in a 1936 toy catalog. $250.00. *Courtesy Kris Lundquist.*

Beautiful mint WENDY ANN BRIDE that is all composition and original. Mohair wig with thick braids curled over ears. Glassene eyes indicate that this doll was made after 1945. In this condition - $700.00 up. *Courtesy Kris Lundquist.*

14" all composition KATE GREENAWAY dressed in unusual tagged outfit. Uses the PRINCESS ELIZABETH mold and will be marked "Princess Elizabeth" on head. In mint condition and all original. $600.00.

Courtesy Jeannie Nespoli.

11" SCARLETT made of composition and is all original. Has paper label on bottom of skirt. In mint condition and in a very rare size. In this condition - $600.00. *Courtesy Patricia Wood.*

This 21" doll was advertised as PRINCESS FLAVIA in 1939. In 1946, she was called VICTORIA. Made of all composition and has extra face makeup. Uses the WENDY ANN doll. All original. $1,800.00 up. *Courtesy Turn of Century Antiques.*

21" MELANIE as she appeared in the 1945–1946 Frost Bros. advertisement. All composition and original. Uses the WENDY ANN doll and has extra face makeup. $2,000.00 up. *Courtesy Turn of Century Antiques.*

21" all composition LADY WINDERMERE, a Portrait from 1945–1946. Has extra face makeup. All original. $1,800.00 up. *Courtesy Susan Giradot.*

21" BRIDESMAID is a very beautiful doll from 1940s. Has glassene sleep eyes, muff, and wrist tag. Mint and all original. In this condition - $1,600.00 up. *Courtesy Jeannie Nespoli.*

14" Sonja Henie in original tagged gold dress. Has brown sleep eyes and mohair wig. Made of all composition. Trunk includes 1939–1940 skating program and original show tickets. **$1,000.00 up.** *Courtesy Ann Wencel.*

18" all composition Sonja Henie with sleep eyes and open mouth. Hair is in original set. Doll and outfit are in mint condition. **$900.00.** *Courtesy Jeannie Nespoli.*

21" Sonja Henie made of all composition with brown sleep eyes. A very pretty all original doll. Dressed in mint condition outfit. **$950.00 up.** *Courtesy Jeannie Nespoli.*

18" all composition Sonja Henie dressed in original skating dress and skates. Muff and hat added but make a nice touch to doll's overall look. **$950.00 up.**
Courtesy Jeannie Nespoli.

21" all composition SONJA HENIE with brown sleep eyes. Dressed in tagged velvet skate outfit, matching tam, and fur cape. Missing gold shoe skates. $950.00 up. *Courtesy Patricia Wood.*

Beautiful 21" MARGARET O'BRIEN with thick braids rolled back in a loop and tied with ribbon. Made of all composition and has sleep eyes. All original. $975.00. *Courtesy Susan Giradot.*

24" SPECIAL GIRL with BETTY face. Composition head and limbs, cloth body. Doll is unmarked but dress is tagged. Mint and all original. In this condition - $585.00. *Courtesy Martha Sweeney.*

13" ALICE IN WONDERLAND using the WENDY ANN face. All composition with jointed waist. Right arm bent at elbow. Has sleep eyes. All original. $400.00 up. *Courtesy Susan Giradot.*

Tony Sarg was the leading puppeteer in the 1930s. His largest puppet show was at the Chicago Fair in 1933. It was seen by more than three million people. It was during this time that industry began using puppets for advertising and public relations.

In the March 1934 *Playthings* magazine, it was reported a line of Tony Sarg marionettes and their theatre were available on the market. The distributor, not the manufacturer, was the Madame Alexander Doll Company.

By June 1937, *Playthings* advertisements listed the following plays and marionettes: "Hansel and Gretel" with Hansel, Gretel, and witch; "Rip Van Winkle" with Rip, Dame, and Judith; "Alice In Wonderland" with Alice, Humpty Dumpty, Tweedle-Dum, and Tweedle-Dee; "Tingling Circus #1" with clown, Zaza, and dog Fido; "Tingling Circus #2" with Riding Master Percival, ballet dancer, and horse. In October 1937, another advertisement listed these plays and characters: "Twinkling Circus" with Sambo, Bones, and Interlocutor; "The Enchanted Prince" with Prince, Princess, and gnome; "The Three Wishes" with Martin, Margaret, and Fairy Titania; "Lucy Lavender's Hero" with Lucy Lawerence and Butler Tippytoes; "Clever Gretchen" with Gretchen and Mr. Archibald; "Red Riding Hood" with Red, Grandmother, and wolf. There were a total of 11 plays and 33 characters.

Advertisements that appeared in 1938 *Playthings* magazines stated Madame Alexander was the exclusive distributor for Tony Sarg's Disney Silly Symphony Theatre. Included with the theatre were marionettes of Mickey and Minnie Mouse. Also available for separate purchase were Donald Duck, Pluto, and Snow White.

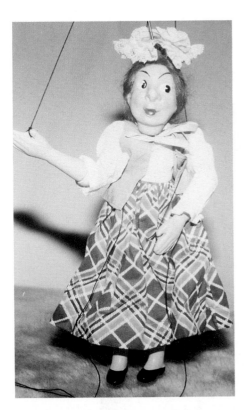

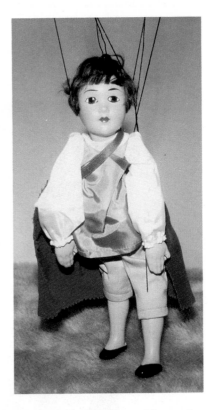

These Tony Sarg marionettes are made of composition and cloth. Each have painted features. Madame Alexander tags are on clothes. Left: This marionette could be several different characters from JUDITH to MARGARET. Possibly Red Riding Hood's GRANDMOTHER, but she should have gray hair and be in night clothes. Center: The wolf from "Red Riding Hood" wearing Grandmother's cape. Right: This prince could have been used for several plays. Each - $265.00–285.00. *Courtesy Susan Giradot.*

21" DEBRA BRIDE that is all hard plastic and uses the MARGARET doll. Extremely elaborate gown with three-tiered bustle from waist in back. Very rare. **$3,000.00 up.** *Courtesy Mary Paine.*

14" GODEY BRIDE from 1949–1950. May be the only Madame Alexander bride with veil that ties under chin. This doll in this condition is scarce. (See other views below.) **$900.00 up.** *Courtesy Mary Paine.*

Left: Another view of GODEY BRIDE. She has center part hairdo pulled forward and up into curls. Right: Back view of gown. Note dress length. *Courtesy Mary Paine.*

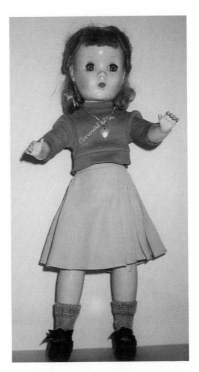

21" MAGGIE made of all hard plastic and wearing pleated skirt dress. Sweater has her name on it. She is all original. This doll is scarce in this outfit and size. $650.00. *Courtesy Jeannie Nespoli.*

14" ANNABELLE using the MAGGIE doll. She is all hard plastic. Her name is embroidered on sweater. Skirt has kick pleats on side. All original. $500.00. *Courtesy Jeannie Nespoli.*

14" all hard plastic STUFFY from *Little Men*. Has paper fashion medal tag on wrist. All original and uses the MAGGIE face. $850.00. *Courtesy Susan Giradot.*

14" all hard plastic NAT from *Little Men*. Uses the MAGGIE face. All original. From 1952. $850.00. *Courtesy Susan Giradot.*

18" all hard plastic KATHY with sleep eyes. Uses the MAGGIE doll. Doll and dress are original and in mint condition. (Hair bows have been replaced.) $775.00.
Courtesy Jeannie Nespoli.

18" red headed MAGGIE dressed in rare tagged outfit. Made of all hard plastic with glassene sleep eyes. In this dress - $700.00. *Courtesy Jeannie Nespoli.*

17" POLLY PIGTAILS using the MAGGIE doll. These hard plastic dolls are things of beauty when outfits and dolls are all original and in mint condition. $85.00.
Courtesy Jeannie Nespoli.

This PRINCESS MARGARET ROSE was shown in the 1946 Ward's catalog as coming in 15", 18", and 21" sizes. The gown came in several pastel shades. Has clover leaf wrist tag. Uses MARGARET face. 18" - $775.00. *Courtesy Susan Giradot.*

14" MEG of LITTLE WOMEN. All hard plastic with wonderful face color. All original. From 1951. $450.00.
Courtesy Kris Lundquist.

14" AMY of *Little Women* Series of 1952–1954. All hard plastic with paper fashion award tag on arm. All original. $475.00. *Courtesy Susan Giradot.*

25" BINNIE BRIDE of 1954–1955. She was a transitional doll to the CISSY doll. (CISSY has vinyl arms jointed at elbows.) BINNIE, WINNIE, and CISSY all have the same general face. Original with wrist tag. $475.00. *Courtesy Kris Lundquist.*

21" CISSY in the 1958 "Lady in Red" classic gown. Mint and original. In this condition and gown - $800.00. *Courtesy Charmaine Shields.*

Left: NURSE Alexander-kin that is a bend knee walker from 1956. Right: Vogue NURSE GINNY. Both dolls are original. ALEXANDER-KIN - $500.00; GINNY - $325.00. *Courtesy Jay Minter.*

8" NURSE Alexander-kin that is all original, including the baby. Bend knee walker. $450.00. *Courtesy Jeannie Mauldin.*

8" straight leg walker ALEXANDER-KIN from 1955. Has very good face color. Mint and original. In this condition - $600.00. *Courtesy Susan Giradot.*

8" bend knee walker ALEXANDER-KIN, mint in box. Made of all hard plastic. In this condition - $325.00. *Courtesy Sandy Johnson Barts.*

10" CISSETTE in original box but missing shoes. Has jointed knees. From late 1950s. In this condition - $325.00. *Courtesy Kris Lundquist.*

10" CISSETTE in mint condition with box. Has wrist tag and brochure of clothing in box. From late 1950s. $325.00. *Courtesy Kris Lundquist.*

All original LITTLE GENIUS in mint condition. Has hard plastic head and body. Limbs are vinyl. From 1960. $275.00 up. *Courtesy Doll Cradle.*

LITTLE GENIUS shown with trunk and wardrobe. Doll is original with wrist tag. This shows some of the outfits that could be purchased separately for the doll. Doll only - $275.00; with wardrobe as shown - $650.00. *Courtesy Kris Lundquist.*

8" LITTLE GENIUS with hard plastic head and lamb's wool wig. Vinyl body and limbs. All original. $275.00. *Courtesy Susan Giradot.*

The Fischer Quints were born in September 1963 in Aberdeen, South Dakota, and were the first quintuplets born in the United States. However, they were not destined to have the popularity that occurred 30 years earlier for the Dionne Quints of Canada, the first surviving set.

The Fischer children consisted of four girls and one boy: Mary Magdalene, Mary Margaret, Mary Anne, Mary Catherine, and James Andrew. Not too long after their birth, it became almost common place for quintuplets to be born around the world. There was even one set of surviving sextuplets.

8" FISCHER QUINTS using the LITTLE GENIUS doll. Hard plastic heads with vinyl bodies and limbs. Original bunting. Each wears original diaper and booties. Set came with one blue and four pink baby bottles tagged "Original Quints." From 1964. In this condition - $485.00.

21" JACQUELINE with brown sleep eyes. Dressed in #2210 "Inauguration" gown. Has original purse over one arm. Mint and all original. A wonderful doll to own. $950.00. *Courtesy Jeannie Nespoli.*

21" JACQUELINE dressed in suit and pill box hat made famous by Mrs. Kennedy. This outfit is found mostly on the 10½" CISSETTE rather than the 21" size. $650.00 up. *Courtesy Jeannie Nespoli.*

15" CAROLINE in riding habit. Doll was made in 1961–1962 only. All original except for replaced shoes. $350.00 up. *Courtesy Jeannie Nespoli.*

21" SHARI LEWIS with high heel feet and hair net. Made in 1958–1959 only. Mint and original. In this outfit and condition - $900.00. *Courtesy Jeannie Nespoli.*

A set of LITTLE WOMEN made for the FAO Schwarz 100th Anniversary in 1962. A wooden horse imprinted with FAO Schwarz logo accompanied doll set. Back row: AMY dressed in blue dress with yellow pinafore and BETH in pink floral print. Front row: MEG dressed in pink dress with blue and white striped pinafore, JO in red dress, and MARMEE in mauve print dress and black apron. Two of these dolls were used from 1957 and the others from 1959. Set - $1,100.00. *Courtesy The Doll Cradle.*

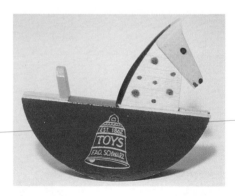

Wooden horse from FAO Schwarz 100th Anniversary that came with the set of LITTLE WOMEN dolls shown above. *Courtesy Doll Cradle.*

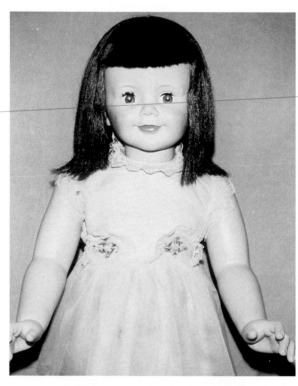

36" JOANIE with flirty sleep eyes with lashes. Head and arms are strung and body has iron rod through it. Made of plastic and vinyl. Original. Marked "Alexander 19©59." $450.00 up. *Courtesy private collection.*

10" JASMIN Portrette from 1987–1988. Uses the CISSETTE doll. $75.00.

10" VIOLETTA Portrette from 1987–1988. $75.00.

10" COLLEEN Portrette from 1988. $75.00.

10" IRIS Portrette from 1988. $75.00.

8" SHEA made especially for the Collector United Doll Show in 1990. $250.00.

10" MISS UNITY made especially for the United Federation of Doll Clubs Madame Alexander luncheon in 1991. MISS UNITY is the U.F.D.C. logo doll. $350.00.

8" MAGGIE MOUSEKETEER made exclusively for Disneyworld, 1991–1993. $95.00.

8" MISS GODEY made exclusively for the Madame Alexander Doll Club in 1992. $165.00.

Back row: TREE TOPPER from 1992, 8" SCARLETT with abnormally large bonnet from 1992. Front row: QUEEN ISABELLA and CHRISTOPHER COLUMBUS from 1992, PINNOCHIO from 1992 to 1995. TOPPER - $65.00; SCARLETT - $75.00; QUEEN - $80.00; COLUMBUS - $80.00; PINOCCHIO - $55.00. *Courtesy Turn of Century Antiques.*

8" CORONATION QUEEN and WENDY LOVES BEING LOVED were second mid-year introductions and then discontinued. From 1992. Queen - $130.00; Wendy - $105.00.

8" COWARDLY LION from 1993, GLENDA THE GOOD WITCH from 1992, and the SCARECROW from 1993. LION - $55.00; GLENDA - $60.00; SCARECROW - $55.00. *Courtesy Turn of Century Antiques.*

10" BLUE FAIRY from 1993, 8" GEPPETO and PINNOCHIO from 1992. FAIRY - $92.00; GEPPETO - $45.00; PINNOCHIO - $55.00. *Courtesy Turn of Century Antiques.*

8" Disneyworld's ROUNDUP COWGIRL. Made exclusively for Disney in 1992. $80.00. *Courtesy Gloria Anderson.*

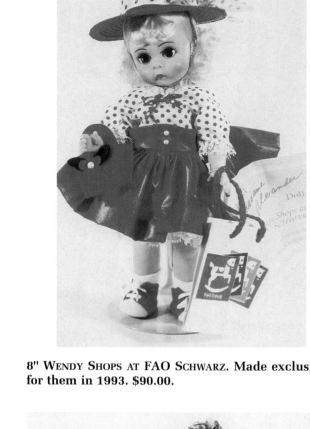

8" WENDY SHOPS AT FAO SCHWARZ. Made exclusively for them in 1993. $90.00.

8" WENDY VISITS WORLD FAIR was made exclusively for Shirley's Doll House to commemorate the 100th anniversary of the Chicago World's Fair. From 1994. $80.00.

10" SCARLETT AT THE BALL dressed all in black. 1992 only. $120.00.

21" MAID MARION is one of the most spectacular dolls created in this size in recent years. She has one long braid that runs through headpiece. Uses JACQUELINE doll. $350.00. *Courtesy Roger Jones.*

21" ENCHANTED EVENING reintroducing the CISSY mold. 1991–1992. $250.00. *Courtesy Roger Jones.*

8" LITTLE DEVIL from the Americana Series. Made in 1992. $55.00.

8" BUMBLE BEE from the Americana Series. Made in 1992–1993. All original. $55.00.

10" SCARLETT IN RED dressed in great gown and boa. Uses CISSETTE doll and has contrasting green sleep eyes. From 1994. $100.00. *Courtesy Roger Jones.*

WENDY AS PATRON OF THE ARTS is I. Magnin's 1994 limited edition doll. She wears a red ribbon and part of the cost of the doll will go to help fight AIDS. She comes with bear and painter's palette. The stand and painting are by Ann Rast and can be ordered with doll. The painting has the bear holding the doll. Doll - $80.00; with stand - $110.00. *Courtesy Margaret Mandel.*

8" NAVAJO LADY is the Madame Alexander Doll Club's convention doll for 1994. The Kachina, basket, sheep, and Indian blanket were part of the entire package. Doll has yellow and blue floral petticoats under the red skirt. Her wig is pulled to side and she has a scarf around head. $300.00. *Courtesy Margaret Mandel.*

13" JACKIE ROBINSON **made by Allied-Grand Doll Mfg. Co., Inc. of Brooklin, NY and copyrighted in 1949. Doll is all composition and original. Shown with a "Play Ball With Jackie Game," a signed wooden bat, a windbreaker with "Dodgers" missing from the front, and a "Jackie's Rise to Fame" booklet in comic book form. Doll - $1,000.00 up.** *Courtesy Amanda Hash.*

American Character

American Character's most noted period was during the 1950s hard plastic era. They dressed their dolls to perfection and when one sees a Sweet Sue, a Toni, a Betsy McCall, or even a baby Tiny Tears in unplayed with condition, it is a beautiful sight.

One of the "forgotten" dolls made by American Character was Tressy. She had a hair growing feature and regular Barbie-style makeup. When styled with pale flesh tones, no heavy makeup or eyelashes, and molded eyelids, Tressy was known as Mary Makeup. This doll came with a makeup kit so the child could "do" the face. Due to Tressy/Mary Makeup clothes fitting Barbie, it is difficult to locate boxed outfits for these dolls. Both dolls were made in 1963.

20" CHUCKLES **of 1928. Composition head and arms with cloth body and legs. Sleep eyes, open mouth. Original dress, shoes and socks replaced. Marked "American Character" on neck. Holds** PRECIOUS MOMENTS **cloth doll with tear on its cheek. $200.00.**
Courtesy Jeannie Mauldin.

12½" PETITE BABY made by American Character in 1920s. Has painted eyes. Doll is all original and in original box. Marked "Petite." In box - $95.00. *Courtesy Pat Graff.*

17" all hard plastic SWEET SUE is a walker doll from 1950. Has eyeshadow wash over eyes. Dressed in 1952 "Sweet Sue Coed" dress. Elastic on sleeves is gone. (Sleeves should be tight and pushed up the arms.) $275.00. *Courtesy Pat Graff.*

SWEET SUE DREAM BRIDE came in sizes from 14" up to 32". Made of all hard plastic. Has inset vinyl scalp with rooted hair that fits into a cut out area in head. Made in 1951–1952. 17" - $275.00. *Courtesy Carol Turpen.*

18" SWEET SUE in very rare outfit called "Mardi Gras" from 1952. By far one of the most beautiful gowns made for this doll. $400.00 up. *Courtesy Jeannie Nespoli.*

18" all hard plastic SWEET SUE dressed in hoop skirt. All original. Made in 1951. $365.00 up. *Courtesy Jeannie Nespoli.*

20" SWEET SUE SOPHISICATE from 1957. Hard plastic doll with vinyl head and rooted hair. Has green sleep eyes. Although it does not look like it, this doll is originally dressed. Outfit is complete with bra, girdle, and hose. $285.00. *Courtesy Pat Graff.*

14" TINY TEARS in suitcase with layette. Hard plastic head with sleep eyes and dark lamb's wool wig. Rubber body. Open mouth nurser. From 1950. Marked "American Character" on head. $145.00.
Courtesy Susan Giradot.

20" all heavy vinyl TOODLES baby with flirty sleep eyes, long lashes, and rooted hair. This romper suit also came in blue and yellow. All original. $175.00.
Courtesy Jeannie Mauldin.

Two 24" and one 30" TOODLES from 1960. All have "Follow Me Eyes" – eyes set in such an oval that they appear to be looking at you from wherever you stand. Open/closed mouth with upper and lower teeth. Doll on right in mint, unplayed with condition. The rest are nicely re-dressed. 24" in unplayed with condition - $250.00; 24" redressed - $150.00. 30" redressed - $200.00. *Courtesy private collection.*

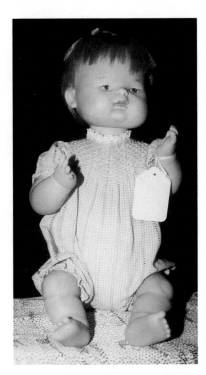

18" TOODLE LOO in original romper suit. Made of all vinyl. Has painted eyes and rooted hair. $185.00.
Courtesy Jeannie Mauldin.

23" CHUCKLES made of plastic and vinyl with painted features. A sweet character and hard to find in this all original condition. In mint condition and has original box. Made in 1961. $185.00 up. *Courtesy Jeannie Mauldin.*

14" POUTY PIXIE with foam body, legs, and upper arms. Wire runs through the foam for posing doll. Vinyl head, rooted hair, and freckles. Very pouty painted features. Marked "Amer. Char. Inc./1968" on head. $25.00. *Courtesy Kathy Tvrdik.*

19" all vinyl WHIMSIE called ANNE THE ASTRONAUT. Has painted features, and on this doll, the gloves and boots are painted on. All original with scarce bubble helmet. From 1960. $100.00 up. *Courtesy Ellyn McCorkell.*

9" DICK TRACY made by Applause. Head, lower arms, and legs are vinyl. The remainder is cloth. Painted features, molded-on hat. Clothes are removable. (See *Modern Collector Dolls, Sixth Series* for "Dick Tracy" characters made by Playmates.) **$22.00.** *Courtesy Kathy Tvrdik.*

BREATHLESS MAHONEY, played by Madonna, from the movie *Dick Tracy*. Cloth and vinyl with molded hair and painted features. **$22.00.** *Courtesy Kathy Tvrdik.*

9" cloth and vinyl PRUNE FACE with painted features. From *Dick Tracy* movie. **$25.00.** *Courtesy Kathy Tvrdik.*

9" cloth and vinyl FLAT TOP from *Dick Tracy* movie. Molded hair and painted features. Eyebrows painted in one line. **$25.00.** *Courtesy Kathy Tvrdik.*

9" cloth and vinyl ITCHY from *Dick Tracy* movie. Has molded hair, painted features, vinyl hat, and molded-on glasses. **$25.00.** *Courtesy Kathy Tvrdik.*

9" cloth and vinyl BIG BOY from *Dick Tracy* movie. Has molded-on hat. Painted features and mustache. **$25.00.** *Courtesy Kathy Tvrdik.*

⮞ Arranbee ⮜

Arranbee was founded in 1922, and was able to compete with other doll companies until 1959, when the company was sold to Vogue Inc. One of their molds was used until 1961 by Vogue as both Wee Imp with red rooted hair and Littlest Angel using the R&B mark. These 10½–11" toddlers are a problem unless they are marked or have red hair. Other companies had the exact same doll, such as Debbie by Nancy Ann Storybook or Suzie Ann by Block Doll Co. All were made from mid-1950s to early 1960s.

Other marks used by Arranbee besides the R&B are "Made in U.S.A." on back and "210" or "250" on head. Teen types were marked Ⓟ.

The majority of Nanettes are in 14" and 17–18" sizes. Nancy Ann dolls are 21" and 23" in size.

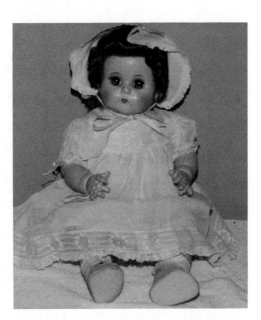

22" LITTLE ANGEL from 1940s. Composition head and limbs, cloth body. Glued on wig and large sleep eyes. All original. Marked "R&B" on head. **$150.00.** *Courtesy Jeannie Mauldin.*

18" all original SONJA SKATER dolls. Doll on left is made of composition; one on right, hard plastic. Both marked "R&B." Each - $350.00 up. *Courtesy Kris Lundquist.*

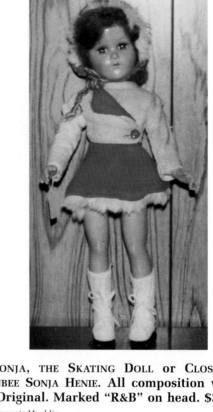

17" SONJA, THE SKATING DOLL or CLOSED MOUTH ARRANBEE SONJA HENIE. All composition with sleep eyes. Original. Marked "R&B" on head. $350.00 up. *Courtesy Jeannie Mauldin.*

8½" LITTLE BO PEEP and DUTCH BOY made of all composition. Both have painted features and modeled hair. Note oversized buttons on the boy. Both are original except BO PEEP *has* lost her one sheep and her staff. Each - $185.00. *Courtesy Patricia Wood.*

18" NANETTE is in mint condition and original in skating costume. All hard plastic with sleep eyes, saran wig, and beautiful face color. In this condtion - $400.00. *Courtesy Jeannie Venner.*

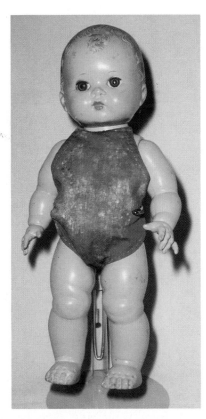

12" all hard plastic toddler DREAM BABY was reintroduced from the composition mold in 1954. Has sleep eyes and hair lashes. $85.00 up. *Courtesy Kathy Tvrdik.*

14" all hard plastic NANETTE COWGIRL from 1954. Original except hat. Original cowboy hat is black pressed felt with white band. $300.00 up. *Courtesy Jeannie Nespoli.*

Very pretty 14" NANETTE GOES SHOPPING. Made of all hard plastic with sleep eyes. All original. In this condition - $300.00 up. *Courtesy Pat Graff.*

14" NANETTE SCHOOL DAY with Dynel wig. All hard plastic with sleep eyes. Has replaced shoes and socks. $300.00 up. *Courtesy Peggy Millhouse.*

18" NANETTE as CINDERELLA with styled floss wig and sleep eyes. Made of all hard plastic. Wears clear "glass" slippers. $400.00. *Courtesy Susan Giradot.*

14" NANETTE wearing an original Shapperilli dress that balloons from waist and then becomes tight around knees. Made of all hard plastic with floss styled wig. $350.00.

21" NANCY ANN is a stunning doll in mint condition. Made of all hard plastic. All original. $465.00. *Courtesy Jeannie Nespoli.*

20" NANCY LEE with styled floss hairdo and sleep eyes. Made of all hard plastic. All original. $465.00.

10" LIL' IMP has rooted hair in a vinyl head, green sleep eyes with molded lashes, and a hard plastic body with jointed knees. A beautiful example of this doll. Mint and original. In this condition - $80.00.
Courtesy Maureen Fukushima.

10" LITTLEST ANGEL dressed in original rain set. Made of all hard plastic with protruding upper lip. Sleep eyes have molded lashes with painted lashes under eyes only. Marked "R&B" on head. $45.00.

⤜ Artisan Novelty Co. ⤛

Artisan Novelty Co. of Gardena, California, began making dolls in 1950. (Their New York office was opened in 1951.) They had both 20" Raving Beauty and Miss Gadabout dolls on the market by 1951. The first dolls made were packaged in a silver tube. Early models may have clothes tagged "California Originals by Michele."

Although the dolls are unmarked, they are easy to recognize because they have a very distinctive look all their own. These dolls have round faces with large sleep eyes, and their legs are far apart. Artisan used both rayon (dynel) and saran wigs. On the hands, the second and third fingers are slightly curled.

20" all hard plastic RAVING BEAUTY walker. Has open mouth with felt tongue and four teeth. Wig made of Swiss fiber. Unmarked. $275.00 up. *Courtesy Susan Giradot.*

20" RAVING BEAUTY COWGIRL represents Annie Oakley. Made of all hard plastic with thick Swiss fiber wig. Brown sleep eyes, open mouth. $365.00. *Courtesy Jeannie Nespoli.*

15½" KEMFY KIDS were sold through A&C Kemfy Kids and made by Astra Trading Corp. in 1985. They have plastic heads, vinyl hands, and cloth bodies. Each came with birth registry certificate. Original. Each - $32.00. *Courtesy Genie Jenright.*

10½" KAR-A-A-ATE by Aurora. Figures kick, chop, and fall when hit on chest. Movements operated from stand. Extra joints except legs. Clothes are removable. Marked "Aurora Prod./1975" on head. Each - $42.00. *Courtesy Don Tvrdik.*

⌒Barbie⌒

Barbie doll's full name is Barbara Millicent Roberts. She lives in Willow, Wisconsin, with her parents, George and Margaret Roberts. Her two younger sisters are Skipper and Tutti, who has a twin brother, Todd. Her best friends are Midge Hadley and Ken Carson. Both she and Ken graduated from Willow High School at age 17 and both went to State College.

If Barbie was a real person, she would weigh 110 lbs., and stand 5' 10" tall. Her measurements would be 39-18-33, and she would wear a size 7 dress.

During the earlier years of overwhelming success, there were 1.5 million members in the Barbie Fan Club, a Mattel organization. At that time, it was the largest girl's club in the world, except for the Girl Scouts.

By 1974, 80 million Barbies were sold, and 90% of girls between ages 5 and 11 owned one or more Barbie dolls. By 1981, the 135-millionth Barbie had been sold.

In 1978, Mattel used between 4 to 5 million yards of fabric for Barbie clothes alone.

Only the #1 and #2 Barbies have inverted "V" eyebrows, and the iris of the eyes are painted white instead of blue. They also have bright red lipstick. There are metal-lined holes in the bottom of the feet to fit the first stands. Prongs on the stands positioned in the holes allowed Barbie to stand. Mint condition - $3,400.00.

The prices listed are for Barbies never removed from box or mint in box dolls. Subtract one-half for any missing a box and subtract another one-fourth if doll or outfit has been played with.

American Girl $1,400.00
Angel Face $30.00
Astronaut... $50.00
Baby Sits, 1963–1965 .... $250.00
    1974–1976 .... $55.00
Baggies (doll in plastic bag) $55.00–95.00
Ballerina $30.00
Beautiful Bride.....................................$200.00
    Hair Lashes $250.00
Beauty Secrets...................................... $40.00
Bendable legs, 1965...$650.00   1966..$900.00
Black.. $45.00
Bubble Cut $275.00
Busy $200.00
Busy Talking $275.00
Color Magic .... $1,000.00 up
Crystal $30.00
Day To Night $25.00
Dream Date.. $30.00
Dream Glow $20.00
Dreamtime.. $15.00
Dressed boxed doll..........................$300.00 up
  Pink Sillouette...........................$800.00 up
  Wedding Day set.....................$1,500.00 up
Eskimo... $150.00

Fashion Jeans $20.00
Fashion Photo $65.00
Fashion Queen $500.00
Feelin' Groovy $140.00
Free Moving.. $65.00
Fun Time $15.00
Gift Giving.. $15.00
Gift sets (NRFB prices)
  Barbie Hostess............................. $2,500.00
  Barbie/Ken Little Theatre............. $2,800.00
  Barbie, Ken & Midge Pep Rally.... $1,700.00
  Barbie, Ken & Midge on Parage ... $2,000.00
  Barbie Movie Groovy (Sears) $350.00
  Barbie Perfectly Plaid (Sears)......... $350.00
  Barbie Round The Clock $950.00
  Barbie Sparkling Pink..................... $950.00
  Barbie Travels In Style (Sears) $700.00
  Barbie & Ken Tennis $1,500.00
  Barbie Color Magic (Sears).......... $1,500.00
  Fashion Queen & Friends............... $700.00
  Fashion Queen & Ken Trousseau .. $1,600.00
  Mix & Match Ponytail $1,200.00
    Bubble Cut $800.00
  Party Set.................................$1,800.00
  Trousseau set............................... $3,000.00
German $75.00
Golden Dream $40.00
Gold Medal $90.00
  Skater... $35.00
  Skier $15.00
Great Shape.. $15.00

Left to right: GREAT SHAPE BARBIE, 1983. **$15.00.** ANGEL FACE BARBIE, 1982. **$30.00.** MAGIC CURL BARBIE, 1981. **$25.00.** *Courtesy Gloria Anderson.*

ALL STAR AEROBIC BARBIE from 1989. Made in China.
$15.00. *Courtesy Kathy Tvrdik.*

CRYSTAL BARBIE with lavender eyes. From 1989.
$30.00. *Courtesy Kathy Tvrdik.*

LOVING YOU BARBIE was on the market in 1983–1984.
$60.00. *Courtesy Kathy Tvrdik.*

MY FIRST BARBIE from 1986. Arms are straight. Note ethnic face on black doll. Each - $25.00. *Courtesy Kathy Tvrdik.*

Growing Pretty Hair, 1971, pink......... $295.00

    1972, blue $295.00

Hair Fair... $85.00

Hair Happenin's...................................... $80.00

Happy Birthday (white or pink) $25.00

Hawaiian $40.00

Hispanic.. $60.00

Horse Lovin' $30.00

India $125.00

Italian $195.00

Japanese $100.00

Jewel Secrets $20.00

Kissing .... $45.00   With bangs $60.00

Live Action ....$150.00   On stage $175.00

Living $175.00

Loving You.. $60.00

Magic Curl Moves................................... $25.00

Malibu, 1971 .... $30.00

Mardi Gras $95.00

Miss Barbie $1,500.00

My First... $25.00

Newport $125.00

Oriental $150.00

Parisian $125.00

Peaches & Cream $30.00

Pink & Pretty.. $35.00

Plus Three.. $50.00

Ponytail:

    #1, blonde....$3,400.00   brunette ..$3,800.00

    #2, blonde....$3,200.00   brunette ..$3,500.00

    #3 ....$800.00

    #4 ....$500.00

    1962–1965 ....$400.00

Pretty Changes $35.00

Quick Curl .... $60.00   Deluxe $75.00

Rocker Barbie, 1986–1987..................... $30.00

Roller Skating $50.00

Royal $250.00

Scottish $150.00

Sears Celebration $60.00

Standard, 1967–1972............................ $325.00

Star N' Stripes.. $60.00

Spanish $115.00

Sun Gold Malibu $18.00

Sun Lovin' $25.00

Sunsational $25.00

Very pretty PEACHES 'N CREAM BARBIE from 1984. $30.00. *Courtesy Kathy Tvrdik.*

BARBIE ROCKER from 1986. Made in the Philippines $30.00. *Courtesy Kathy Tvrdik.*

Sun Valley	$150.00
Super Hair	$20.00
Super Size Bride	$165.00
Super Hair	$150.00
Super Star	$150.00
Super Star Fashion: Change Abouts	$90.00
In The Spotlight	$70.00
Swedish	$75.00
Sweet Sixteen	$65.00
Swirl Ponytail, platinum blonde	$400.00
Ash blonde	$350.00
Auburn	$450.00
Talking .... $275.00 Spanish	$300.00
Spanish	$300.00
Tropical	$15.00
Twirly Curl	$25.00
Twist N' Turn	$300.00
Walk Lively	$195.00
Ward's Anniversary	$600.00
Western	$20.00
Wig Wardrobe	$195.00

SPECIAL EDITIONS AND STORE SPECIALS

Does not include all, just ones that are most likely to increase in value at a steady rate.

1988:

Equestrienne (Toys Я' Us)	$45.00
Lilac & Lovely (Sears)	$45.00
Mardi Gras	$85.00
Tennis Barbie & Ken (Toys Я' Us)	$40.00
Sweet Dreams (Toys Я' Us)	$35.00

1989:

Army	$30.00
Dance Club (Child's World)	$45.00
Denim Deluxe (Toys Я' Us)	$25.00
Evening Enchantment (Sears)	$45.00
Golden Greeting (FAO Schwarz)	$150.00
Gold n' Glitter (Target)	$35.00
Lavender Look (Wal-Mart)	$25.00
Party Lace (Hills)	$25.00
Party Pink (Winn-Dixie)	$20.00
Peach Pretty (K-Mart)	$40.00

DANCE CLUB BARBIE came with tape cassette. From 1989. $15.00. *Courtesy Kathy Tvrdik.*

PEACH PRETTY BARBIE from 1989. Hair is fanned out and sewn to box. $35.00. *Courtesy Kathy Tvrdik.*

Pepsi Set (Toys Я' Us) $35.00
Pink Jubilee $1,500.00
Special Expressions (Woolworth) $18.00
Sweet Roses (Toys Я' Us) $25.00
Sweet Treats (Toys Я' Us) $35.00
UNICEF (four nations) .... each $35.00

1990:
Air Force $35.00
Barbie Style (Applause) $35.00
Dance Magic set $45.00
Disney's Barbie (Child's World) $35.00
Dream Fantasy (Wal-Mart) $25.00
Evening Sparkle (Hills) $30.00
Party Sensation (Wholesale Clubs) $75.00
Pink Sensation (Winn-Dixie) $20.00
Special Expressions (2nd, Woolworth) .. $15.00
Summit (four nations) .... each $35.00
Wedding Fantasy $30.00
Western Fun-Sun Runner gift set $55.00
Winter Fantasy (FAO Schwarz) $150.00

1991
All American (Wholesale Clubs) $55.00
Ballroom Beauty (Wal-Mart) $20.00
Barbie Collector Doll (Applause) $35.00
Barbie & Friends Gift Set
    (Disney, Toys Я' Us) $55.00
Blossom Beauty (Shopko/Venture) $25.00
Blue Rhapsody (Service Merchandise) .. $25.00
Cute & Cool (Target) $20.00
Dream Bride $40.00
Enchanted Evening (J.C. Penney) $25.00
Golden Evening (Target) $20.00
Jewel Jubilee (Sam's Club) $35.00
Moonlight & Roses (Hills) $20.00
Navy $20.00
Night Sensation (FAO Schwarz) $135.00
Party In Pink (Ames) $20.00
School Fun (Toys Я' Us) $25.00
Southern Beauty (Winn-Dixie) $20.00
Southern Belle (Sears) $35.00

WEDDING FANTASY BARBIE from 1989. Also came in white version. Made in China. $30.00. *Courtesy Kathy Tvrdik.*

Star Stepper Gift Set
(Wholesale Clubs) $55.00
Sterling Wishes (Spiegel) $95.00
Swan Lake Gift Set (Wholesale Clubs).. $55.00
Sweet Romance (Toys Я' Us) $25.00

1992
Anniversary Star (Wal-Mart) $35.00
Barbie For President (Toys Я' Us) $20.00
Blossom Beauty (Sears) $55.00
Blue Elegance (Hills) $20.00
Cool Look (Toys Я' Us) $20.00
Cool 'N Sassy (Toys Я' Us) $20.00
Dazzlin' Date (Target) $25.00
Denim 'N Lace (Ames) $30.00
Evening Flame (Home Shopping Club).. $30.00
Evening Sensation (J.C. Penney) $28.00
Dr. Barbie (Toys Я' Us) $20.00
Fantastica (Pace) $35.00
Hot Looks (Ames) $25.00
Madison Avenue (FAO Schwarz) $75.00
Marine Corp. $20.00
Marine Barbie & Ken Gift Set $45.00
My Size (3-feet tall) $140.00
Nutcracker $110.00
Party Premiere (Supermarkets) $20.00
Party Perfect (Shopko/Venture) $27.00
Peach Blossoms (Sam's Club) $25.00
Picnic Pretty (Osco) $20.00
Pretty In Plaid (Target) $25.00
Pretty In Purple (K-Mart) $22.00
Radiant In Red (Toys Я' Us) $35.00
Regal Reflections (Spiegel) $95.00
Royal Romance (Price Clubs) $50.00
Satin Nights (Service Merchandise) $35.00
School Fun (Toys Я' Us) $20.00
Something Extra (Meijers) $20.00
Special Expressions (Woolworth) $25.00
Special Parade (Toys Я' Us) $20.00
Sweet Lavender (Woolworth) $23.00
Very Violet (Pace) $40.00
Wild Style (Target) $20.00

1993
Army Desert Storm $20.00
Army Barbie & Ken Gift Set $45.00
Back To School (Supermarkets) $20.00
Baseball (Target) $20.00
Country Looks (Ames) $25.00

Disney Fun (Disney) $30.00
Festiva (Ames) $30.00
Gibson Girl $60.00
Golf Date (Target) $20.00
Golden Winter (J.C. Penney) $25.00
Holiday Hostess (Supermarket) $20.00
Hollywood Hair Gift Set
(Wholesale Clubs) $30.00
Island Fun Gift Set (Wholesale Clubs).. $20.00
Love To Read (Toys Я' Us) $25.00
Little Debbie (Little Debbie Cakes) $35.00
Malt Shop (Toys Я' Us) $20.00
Moonlight Magic (Toys Я' Us) $35.00
1920s Flapper $60.00
Paint 'N Dazzle Gift Set
(Wholesale Clubs) $30.00
Police Officer (Toys Я' Us) $20.00
Radiant In Red (Toys Я' Us) $30.00
Rockette (FAO Schwarz) $85.00
Romantic Bride $35.00
Royal Invitation (Spiegel) $50.00
School Spirit (Toys Я' Us) $20.00
Secret Hearts Gift Set
(Wholesale Clubs) $20.00
Shopping Fun (Meijer) $22.00
Special Expressions (Woolworth) $18.00
Sparkling Splender
(Service Merchandise) $35.00
Spring Bouquet (Supermarkets) $20.00
Spots 'N Dots (Toys Я' Us) $22.00
Super Star (Wal-Mart) $20.00
Western Horse Gift Set (Toys Я' Us) $50.00
Western Stampin' Gift Set
(Wholesale Clubs) $50.00
Winter Royal (Wholesale Clubs) $20.00
Winter Princess (Home Shopping Club).. $70.00

BOB MACKIE COLLECTION
Designer Gold, 1990 .... $600.00
Platinum, 1991 .... $450.00
Starlight Splender, 1991 .... $450.00
Empress Bride, 1992 .... $375.00
Neptune's Daughter, 1992 .... $375.00
Masquerade Ball (Harlequin), 1993 .... $250.00

OTHER DESIGNERS
BillyBoy™ .... $250.00 up

Benefit Ball, Carol Spencer, 1992 .... $60.00
Opening Night, Janet Goldblatt, 1993... $60.00
City Style, Janet Goldblatt, 1993 .... $60.00

HAPPY HOLIDAY BARBIE

1988			....	$400.00
1989			....	$110.00
1990	white	$95.00	black	$75.00
1991	white	$75.00	black	$55.00
1992	white	$65.00	black	$50.00
1993	white or black		....	$38.00

CLOTHING, 1959–1963

After Five $100.00
Apple print sheath.................... $125.00
American Airlines $175.00
Ballerina............................... $150.00
Barbie Baby Sits, with apron $250.00
    With layette........................$300.00
Barbie-Q outfit $125.00
Bride's Dream......................... $175.00
Busy Gal $300.00
Busy Morning $225.00
Candy Striper......................... $350.00
Career Girl............................ $250.00
Cheerleader $175.00
Commuter Set $600.00
Cotton Casual......................... $125.00
Cruise Stripe Dress $125.00
Dinner At Eight....................... $200.00
Drum Majorette....................... $150.00
Easter Parade......................... $2,000.00
Enchanted Evening.................... $250.00
Evening Splendor $175.00
Fancy Free............................. $95.00
Fashion undergarments................ $125.00
Floral petticoat....................... $125.00
Friday Night........................... $200.00
Garden Party $95.00
Gay Parisienne $1,600.00
Golden Elegance $200.00
Golden Girl $195.00
Graduation $50.00
Icebreaker............................. $125.00
It's Cold Outside $125.00
Knitting Pretty Blue ..$350.00 Pink ..$300.00
Let's Dance $125.00

Masquerade $150.00
Mood For Music $125.00
Movie Date $100.00
Nighty-Negligee $125.00
Open Road $250.00
Orange Blossom $100.00
Party Date............................ $150.00
Peachy Fleecy Coat................... $95.00
Picnic Set $250.00
Plantation Belle $300.00
Red Flair.............................. $125.00
Registered Nurse...................... $150.00
Resort Set $125.00
Roman Holiday $1,800.00
Senior Prom $175.00
Sheath Sensation $100.00
Silken Flame $125.00
Singing In The Shower................ $75.00
Ski Queen............................. $125.00
Solo In The Spotlight $275.00
Sophisticated Lady $250.00

Brunette #3 BARBIE wearing "Wedding Day." Doll - $1,000.00 up; outfit only- $350.00. *Courtesy Susan Giradot.*

Sorority Meeting	$175.00
Stormy Weather	$75.00
Suburban Shopper	$200.00
Sweater Girl	$125.00
Sweet Dreams	$175.00
Swingin' Easy	$125.00
Tennis Anyone	$50.00
Theatre Date	$125.00
Wedding Day Set	$350.00
Winter Holiday	$175.00

CLOTHING, 1964–1966

Aboard Ship	$250.00
Beautiful Bride	$800.00
Beau Time	$225.00
Benefit Performance	$850.00
Black Magic	$250.00
Brunch Time	$250.00
Campus Sweetheart	$600.00
Caribbean Cruise	$150.00

AMERICAN GIRL BARBIE with bendable knees. Wearing "Saturday Matinee." Doll - $1,400.00; outfit - $700.00. *Courtesy Susan Giradot.*

Club Meeting	$250.00
Country Club Dance	$300.00
Country Fair	$125.00
Crisp 'N Cool	$140.00
Dancing Doll	$350.00
Debutante Ball	$450.00
Disc Date	$225.00
Dogs 'N Suds	$250.00
Dreamland	$125.00
Evening Enchantment	$475.00
Evening Gala	$275.00
Fabulous Fashion	$475.00
Fashion Editor	$300.00
Fashion Luncheon	$600.00
Floating Gardens	$400.00
Formal Occasion	$450.00
Fraternity Dance	$425.00
Fun At The Fair	$230.00
Fun 'N Games	$230.00
Garden Tea Party	$125.00
Garden Wedding	$370.00
Golden Evening	$185.00
Golden Glory	$295.00
Gold 'N Glamour	$800.00
Here Comes The Bride	$900.00
Holiday Dance	$395.00
International Fair	$375.00
Invitation To Tea	$350.00
Junior Designer	$250.00
Junior Prom	$425.00
Knit Hit	$125.00
Knit Separates	$125.00
Little Theater:	
Abrabian Nights	$275.00
Cinderella	$295.00
Guinevere	$225.00
Red Riding Hood/Wolf	$400.00
London Tour	$295.00
Lunch Date	$90.00
Lunch On The Terrace	$250.00
Lunchtime	$200.00
Magnificence	$450.00
Matinee Fashion	$350.00
Midnight Blue	$500.00
Miss Astronaut	$750.00
Modern Art	$325.00
Music Center Matinee	$500.00
On The Avenue	$400.00

Outdoor Art Show $375.00
Outdoor Life.................................... $200.00
Pajama Party $85.00
Pan Am Airways............................. $2,000.00
Poodle Parade $550.00
Pretty As A Picture............................ $350.00
Reception Line.................................. $385.00
Riding In The Park $400.00
Satin 'N Rose.................................... $250.00
Saturday Matinee............................... $700.00
Shimmering Magic $1,500.00
Skater's Waltz.................................... $285.00
Skin Diver $100.00
Sleeping Pretty.................................. $200.00
Sleeptytime Gal $225.00
Slumber Party $200.00
Sorority Tea...................................... $175.00
Student Teacher................................ $275.00
Sunday Visit..................................... $350.00
Travel outfits:
    Hawaii $200.00
    Holland....................................... $200.00
    Japan.. $375.00
    Mexico.. $200.00
    Switzerland $200.00
Underfashions................................... $350.00
Vacation Time $200.00
White Magic..................................... $185.00

THE MODERATO ERA, 1967–1971

There were an overwhelming number of outfits produced during these years, but many of them are beginning to increase in value at a fast pace. This era of clothing is broken down as follows:

1. Plain street length dresses that have only a few accessories such as Knit Hit, Midi Magic, Snap Dash, etc. $75.00 up.
2. Formals and brides such as Let's Have A Ball, Romantic Ruffles, Silver Serenade, Winter Wedding, etc. $175.00 up.

THE YEARS OF FEARS, 1972–1976

Barbie clothes were of poor quality during these years. The ones that will continue to climb in value are the ones that reflect the times, such as granny dresses, bell bottoms, peasant dresses, and clothes with the "flower child" look. Most are priced between $20.00–45.00.

THE VIGOROUS ERA, 1980–1990s

Most are only worth what you purchased them for, but you should try to keep your collection current and they will rise in value as time goes by. The following have increased in value:

Collector Series .... $45.00 up
Oscar de la Renta Collector Series .. $45.00 up
Teen Talk .... $25.00 up
Benefit Ball $20.00
Rappin' Rockin' $15.00
Sparkle Eyes.................................... $20.00
Flapper $25.00
Gibson $25.00
Troll.. $20.00
Western Stampin' $15.00
Secret Hearts $15.00
Earring Magic................................... $20.00
Roller Blades $50.00

Issued in 1992, but found to be dangerous in July 1994. If doll was skated while hairspray was used, sparks from the blade wheels could ignite the hairspray.

1988–1989

These dolls are important due to number of doll produced.

Perfume Pretty, white or black, 1988.... $25.00
Sensations $25.00
Island Fun, 1988................................. $15.00
Dr. Barbie, 1988 .... $25.00
California Dream, 1988......................... $20.00
Fun To Dress, 1988....$15.00   black $20.00
Feeling Fun, 1988 .... $20.00
My First Barbie, Hispanic, 1988 .... $15.00
Animal Lovin', 1989............................ $20.00
Beach Blast, 1989................................ $15.00
Cool Times, 1989 .... $20.00
Dance Club, 1989............................... $15.00
Garden Party, 1989 .... $20.00
Gift Giving, 1989................................ $15.00
Style Magic, 1989 .... $25.00
Super Star, 1989 ....$20.00   black $20.00

INTERNATIONALS, 1980–1989
(Also see regular listing.)

Canada.. $45.00
Eskimo.. $150.00
German.. $55.00

Greek	$100.00	Scottish	$165.00
Hispanic	$65.00	Spanish	$300.00
Iceland	$85.00	Swedish	$75.00
India	$90.00	Swiss	$75.00
Irish	$70.00		
Italian	$195.00		
Japanese	$100.00		
Korea	$55.00		
Mexico	$100.00		
Oriental	$150.00		
Parisian	$125.00		
Peruvian	$150.00		
Royal (England)	$125.00		
Russia	$125.00		

PORCELAINS

Blue Rhapsody, 1986
   (Limited to 6,000) $700.00
Enchanted Evening, 1987
   (Limited to 10,000) $500.00
Benefit Performance, 1988
   (Limited to 10,000) $365.00
Wedding Party, 1989
   (Limited to 10,000) $450.00

 Lilli

In 1955, the Hamburg, Germany, newspaper *Bild-Bericht* had a cartoon character named "Lilli" that represented everything in "ultra fashion" as did our own "Brenda Starr." By 1957, there was an 11½" Lilli on the market and shown at the Nuremberg Toy Fair. She was made of all plastic with scalp cut out and hair inset. She had molded flower earrings. Her hair was slicked back into a ponytail which was curled on the end and tied. She came with both a spit curl on her forehead and without. She had high arched eyebrows and 1930s Marlene Dietrich-style eye make-up. She had holes on the bottom of ther feet that fit into a round doll stand. The doll stand had "Lilli" on the front and the doll was unmarked. Most dolls were blondes, but brunettes and auburn haired dolls were also made.

The very first Lilli dolls had just one side of the irises painted white. The last design of 1960 had the iris painted around the entire pupil and the basic doll was dressed in a black and white striped swimsuit. She had high heel feet with the shoes painted on.

The Lilli molds were sold to a British Hong Kong firm, Dura-Fam Ltd., which produced the 11½" doll exactly as before, except for the mark "Hong Kong Ⓕ." They also leased a set of molds to Chang-Pi Su Co. who reduced them to a 7½–8" size and dressed, packaged, and marketed them as "Cherie."

The original holder of the molds also sold "blanks" to whomever wanted them. The firms purchasing the blanks then dressed and marketed them as their own. These companies included FAB-LU (Luften, Ltd.), who called her "Babs" as their answer to Mattel's Barbie. Marx, who called their version "Bonnie," amazingly found a way to produce this doll in a 15" size and named her "Miss Seventeen." Other molds were sold to the Australian firm Haro-Mate Ltd. If the dolls were produced in their factory, they were still marked "Hong Kong." They also carried the registration number "British Patent #804566 and U.S. patent #2925684." Another firm, Shak Ind., Inc., marketed their doll as "Babbie." All the Hong Kong dolls apparently were dressed with fashionable outfits that were very comparable to Barbie's.

Because of the relationship between all these dolls, it is difficult for the collector to be sure what they have. If you find an 11½" unmarked Lilli, it may be a *real* German Lilli. The only way you will be certain is to locate an all original doll with stand. Be prepared to paid a small fortune!

11½" LILLI was made in Germany in 1957. Her eyes are to the side and the irises are only partly painted. Molded eyelids. Blonde inset hair set in ponytail. Painted-on shoes. Has holes in bottom of feet for round stand. $650.00 up. *Courtesy Kathy Tvrdik.*

One of the last LILLI dolls on the market in 1960. Note the bathing suit with mismatched stripes and sunglasses. LILLI is copying BARBIE at this date. $700.00 up. *Courtesy David Spurgeon.*

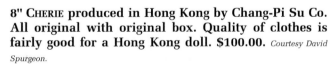

8" CHERIE produced in Hong Kong by Chang-Pi Su Co. All original with original box. Quality of clothes is fairly good for a Hong Kong doll. $100.00. *Courtesy David Spurgeon.*

15" MISS SEVENTEEN made by Marx. All rigid plastic with painted features. Had a very large selection of clothes available. With box - $125.00; mint doll only - $100.00. *Courtesy Sharon McDowell.*

11½" BONNIE made for Marx. Taken from the LILLI molds. Clothes are of very good quality. (See introduction for details.) $600.00.

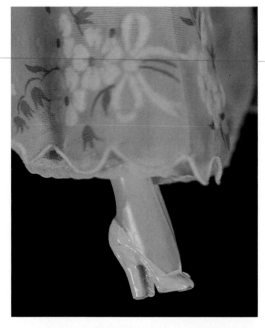

This shows the profile of the shoes on the 11½ BONNIE made by Marx. The painting of the Hong Kong dolls did not equal the quality of the German-made LILLI.

This shows the holes in the bottom of the feet of Marx dressed BONNIE. She was one of the BARBIE copies using the German mold for LILLI. Made in Hong Kong.

7½" Hong Kong LILLI shown with original black stand and box with wardrobe. As with the German LILLI, brunette, black, or red haired dolls are harder to find and more valuable. With box and wardrobe - $125.00 up. *Courtesy David Spurgeon.*

⁓ Betsy McCall ⁓

BESTY McCALL BALLERINAS made by American Character. Sleep eyes, molded lashes, and jointed knees. Can have rooted hair in vinyl cap glued to head or full wig. Left to right: Pink from 1958, red (rare in good condition) from 1957, white from after 1960, and green from 1959–1960. Each - $200.00. *Courtesy Peggy Pergande.*

8" hard plastic BETSY McCALL surrounded by many original articles of clothing. Doll only - $225.00; with this wardrobe - $600.00. *Courtesy Kris Lundquist.*

Packaged clothes for BETSY McCALL. Lid folds down to make box. Box has a window so clothes can be seen. In box - $45.00. *Courtesy Maureen Fukushima.*

8" BETSY McCALL in 1960 dress made of flocked nylon. Socks are missing. Original shoes are extremely difficult to find and expensive. $185.00.
Courtesy Pat Graff.

8" original BETSY McCALL dolls made by American Character. All hard plastic with jointed knees. Marked "Betsy McCall/McCall Corp." Ballgown - $225.00; riding habit - $200.00; dress - $175.00.

8" BETSY McCALL dressed in teddy and shoes. Many dolls were sold this way, then the customer could purchase clothes separately. Basic doll in box - $160.00. *Courtesy Maureen Fukushima.*

This peignoir set also came in lavender and pale green. Came with strap slippers. Both are original. Each - $150.00. *Courtesy Maureen Fukushima.*

"April Showers" makes a pretty outfit on a brunette BETSY McCALL. From 1959. $185.00.

A very beautiful ballgown for a 1958 BETTY McCALL. In this gown - $265.00. *Courtesy Maureen Fukushima.*

All original BETSY McCALL made by American Character. Original socks are like chiffon net or nylon net. $155.00.

8" BETSY McCALL is all original but is missing her shoes. $125.00.

8" BETSY McCALL in "Glamor Girl" from 1966. Note the two different versions. These outfits came in bubble packs. Each - $125.00. *Courtesy Peggy Pergande.*

14" BETSY McCALL with all hard plastic body and vinyl head. Made by Ideal and marked "P–90." From 1952. Mint condition - $295.00.

14" BETSY McCALL made by American Character. Vinyl with rooted hair and round sleep eyes. Marked "McCall Corp. 1958." Mint condition - $265.00. *Courtesy Phyllis Houston-Kates.*

20" BETSY McCALL with flirty eyes made by American Character. Her original outfit is very hard to find. From 1958. $285.00 up. *Courtesy Ann Wencel.*

36" BETSY McCALL and her brother called SANDY by collectors. (His name was actually James in *McCall's* Magazine.) Made by Ideal and marked "McCall 1959." BETSY - $550.00; SANDY/JAMES - $700.00. *Courtesy Sally Bethschieder.*

Left: 12" POOR PITIFUL PEARL who is mint with original box, extra outfit, and book. Shown with 17" in fair condition. Both made by Brookglad in 1957. Center: 15" HARRIET HUBBARD AYER made by Ideal. All original and mint in box. 12" - $250.00; 17" - $95.00; 15"- $325.00. *Courtesy Turn of Century Antiques.*

13" all hard plastic BUDDY LEE dressed in one of his all original cowboy outfits. Marked with his name across the back. $350.00. *Courtesy Susan Giradot.*

 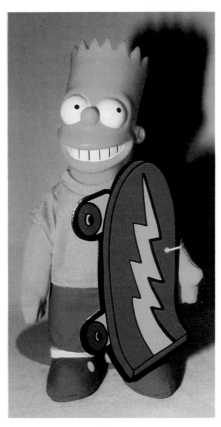 

THE SIMPSONS made for Burger King Corp. in China. Marked "Matt Groening/1990/20th Century Fox F.C." Top row, left to right: 11" HOMER, 9" BART, and 12" MARGE. Bottom row: 9" LISA and 7" MAGGIE. Each - $12.00. *Courtesy Kathy Tvrdik.*

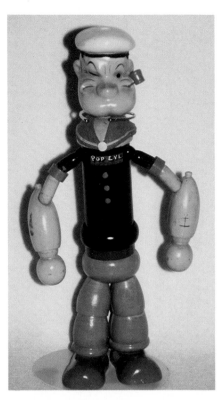

17" POPEYE made by Cameo in 1935. Wooden segmented body with composition head and wooden pipe. The Cameo figure can be distinguished by the jointing of the upper arm (very small) into the lower arm. $500.00. *Courtesy Carol Turpen.*

Left to right: 17" vinyl MARGIE from 1958. Fully jointed with rooted hair and sleep eyes. Marked with name on head and "Cameo" on back. 10" MARGIE from 1929 with composition head, molded hair, and wooden segmented body. Sticker on front. 15" JOY from 1932 with sticker on front. Composition head with molded loop. Wooden segmented legs and arms. Composition body and hands. 17" - $85.00; 10" - $325.00; 15" - $425.00. *Courtesy Jeannie Mauldin.*

15" all composition SCOOTLES. Doll is in such mint condition that it still has its matte finish. Came in original plain cardboard box. Missing matching dress and bonnet. Shown in 1946 Wards catalog. $525.00. *Courtesy Jeannie Mauldin.*

12" all hard plastic KEWPIE with sleep eyes. Uses the same body and hands as SCOOTLES, but feet are less detailed. Note added roll at ankle. Rare doll. $250.00 up. *Courtesy Susan Giradot.*

15" all vinyl KEWPIE made by Cameo. All original. Date is unknown but from about 1960. Note two tags on clothes as shown below: "Kewpie Klothes by Johnston" and "Little People Floor/Lord & Taylor/Fifth Avenue." $165.00. *Courtesy Doll Cradle.*

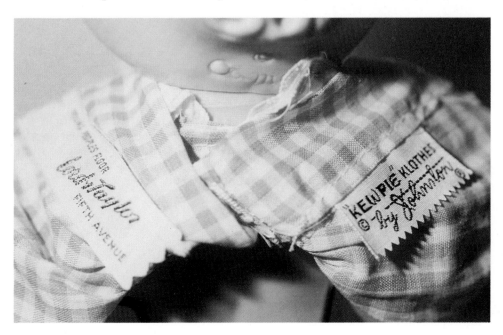

 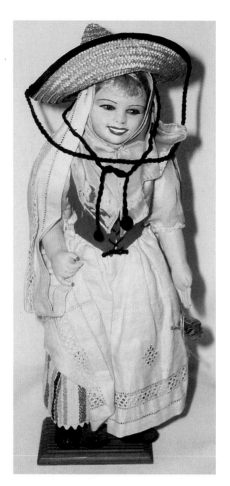

16" man and 15" woman representing the Basque people. A wonderful pair with formed face masks that are hand painted. Tagged "Fataga Las Palmas." Both on wooden bases. Circa 1930s. Each - $300.00.

Delightful 22" Russian tea cozy with heavy solid brass pan. All cloth with heavy quilted skirt underneath clothes. Formed oil-painted face and mitt hands. Offered by Kimport Dolls as "Made in Russia" in 1962 and stored in an American warehouse until now. $100.00.

"Eloise" was born in the mind of Kay Thompson who wrote books about a little girl who lived in New York's Plaza Hotel. The illustrator for the books, Hillary Knight, was asked to do a painting of Eloise for the lobby of the Plaza. Thanks to the special interest and the sense of humor of another famous occupant of the hotel, Ivana Trump, the painting still hangs there today. In 1955, Neiman-Marcus featured the painting on the cover of their Christmas catalog. The Eloise doll was copyrighted by Eloise Ltd. and was made by Hol-le Toy Co. of New York. Bette Gould was her designer.

In 1958, Eloise was reintroduced by the same company wearing a plaid pleated skirt with shoulder straps. She was featured in the 1958 Neiman-Marcus catalog but its success was limited the second time around.

Jacqueline Halcomb pictured with the painting of "Eloise" at the famous Plaza Hotel in New York. The painting has been in one of the lobbies for 40 years.

20" all cloth ELOISE from the 1950s. Designed by Betty Gould and made by the American Character Doll Company. ELOISE is the character from children's books by Kay Thompson. Mint condition - $400.00.

Courtesy Jeannie Mauldin.

ELOISE shown in her Christmas tree dress. A very rare doll. In mint condition - $600.00. *Courtesy Susan Giradot.*

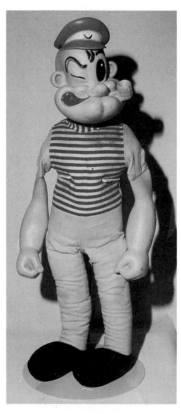

19" cloth and vinyl POPEYE with molded hat and pipe. Marked "411 King Features Sny., Inc./Popeye." $50.00.

20" DEVIL, the alter ego of Mr. Wilson (Gale Gordon) from the "Dennis the Mence" TV show starring Jay North. All satin with plastic face mask and cloth tail. Tagged "Samet & Wells, Inc. New York." From 1959. $45.00.

18" SPARKLING GOLLIWOG made by Dean's Childsplay Toy from 1980s. Lightweight material with printed features. Clothes are felt. $55.00.

Top row: 3" FREDDIE FLINTSTONE with alligator skateboard. WILMA in Sleighhoople-Mastadon rider. Bottom row: BARNEY RUBBLE with soapbox racer. BETTY with sea serpent scooter. Not shown: 3" DINO with wagon. All marked "Coleco 1986. Hanna Barbera Productions, Inc." Each - $9.00.

⌒ Cosmopolitan ⌒

The main reason that Cosmopolitan's Ginger is so popular is the company tagged the clothes and put out many booklets showing the clothes along with order number and name of outfit or series.

Ginger is 7½–8" tall and is found as an all hard plastic walker or non walker. She also came as a bend knee walker with hard plastic body and vinyl limbs. Later models had vinyl heads. She has large round eyes with painted lashes. Some came with the regular 8" doll size eyes. Her feet were flat and bare, but some had "cha-cha" feet which are medium heeled. All Ginger dolls have wide spread legs. Many Ginger doll were sold to other companies to dress and market. Those dolls were sold under other names.

Some of Ginger's characterisitics are a very faint navel, the mold seam runs through the middle of the ear, a dimple under the lower lip, and the toes are the same length and have dots above the toes. All fingers are separated with flaw at wrist on palms. The jointed knee doll has a crease in front ankle. See *Modern Collector Dolls, Fourth Series* on page 8 for comparison study. Also see Disney section.

GINGER FRONTIER LADY from the Frontier set of 1954. Purse does not go with outfit. $80.00. *Courtesy Maureen Fukushima.*

Left to right: 10½" MISS GINGER with vinyl head and rigid vinyl body and limbs. Has rooted hair, sleep eyes, jointed waist, and high heel feet. Marked on head. 7½" all hard plastic GINGER walker. Head turns as she walks. 8" LITTLE MISS GINGER with hard plastic body and vinyl head. No eye lashes. Thighs are heavy. Wears medium heels. From 1957. 10½" - $75.00 up; 7½" - $50.00 up; 8" - $60.00 up. *Courtesy Maureen Fukushima.*

Mint in box MINDY that is actually a GINGER. Blank (nude) dolls were sold to Active Doll Co., and in 1955, they attempted to enter the "beat Ginny" race by making a look-alike of their own. The result is a GINGER in a MINDY outfit. Mint in box - $85.00 up.

Courtesy Kris Lundquist.

PAM produced by Cosmopolitan and sold to Fortune. They also marketed the doll as PAM. As a blank, this same doll was dressed by Virga (Beehler Arts Co.) and sold as LUCY. Doll has fat body, t-strap shoes molded on, and a crease in center of kneecap. Seam lines cut through back of ears. Molded hair under wig. Deep indentation under lower lip (no dimple). This doll is a PAM marketed by Fortune Toys and is mint and complete. From 1954. $75.00. *Courtesy Peggy Millhouse.*

7½" GINGER dressed in outfit #443 from 1955. Unusual center part wig. Mint condition - $65.00.

Courtesy Maureen Fukushima.

GINGER with dark brunette wig and wearing outfit #444 from 1955. Mint and complete. $65.00. *Courtesy Maureen Fukushima.*

7½" GINGER in one of her most desirable outfits. It is also one of the best made and designed outfits for her. MISS GINGER and LITTLE MISS GINGER have matching outfits. From 1956. 7½" - $85.00; 10½" - $115.00. *Courtesy Maureen Fukushima.*

7½" GINGER that is all hard plastic and has bend knees. All original and in mint condition. From late 1950s. $60.00. *Courtesy Pat Graff.*

A cute GINGER ROLLER SKATER with name on bodysuit. Skirt is felt and she wears matching tam. Boot style skates. $65.00. *Courtesy Maureen Fukushima.*

GINGER dressed in her Sunday best. Pink and black is a good color combination for this doll. Mint and all original. $65.00. *Courtesy Maureen Fukushima.*

A very pretty 8" GINGER from the mid-1950s. All hard plastic. All original except for shoes. $65.00. *Courtesy Patricia Wood.*

A beautiful all hard plastic GINGER. Pre-1957. Mint condition - $60.00. *Courtesy Maureen Fukushima.*

8" GINGER in Character Series #665. $65.00. *Courtesy Maureen Fukushima.*

7½" GINGER with hard plastic walker body. Vinyl head with rooted hair. Round sleep eyes with molded lashes. Replaced shoes. $50.00. *Courtesy Kathy Tvrdik.*

Both of these dolls were made by Cosmopolitan and sold to Terri Lee Corp. to dress and distribute. Left: GINGER BROWNIE SCOUT in official uniform with original box. Doll has gold socks. Mint condition - $75.00 up. Right: Another GINGER BROWNIE SCOUT doll, but this one has dark brown socks. Mint in box - $75.00 up. *Courtesy Maureen Fukushima and Jeanne Venner.*

8" FAB DOLL (GINGER) shown with order blank advertisement for Fab Detergent. All hard plastic walker. Head turns when she walks. Has sleep eyes. $60.00.

Courtesy Carol Turpen.

7" all vinyl BABY GINGER with round sleep eyes and rooted hair. Marked with her name on head. All original and in excellent condition. $35.00. *Courtesy Pat Graff.*

Top: GINGER GIFT SET #1701. Named in booklet that comes with doll "The Darling of the Doll World." $100.00 up. Bottom: Case with GINGER luggage. Each piece has her name on it. $35.00. *Courtesy Maureen Fukushima.*

Daddy's Long Legs

The KVK, Inc. of Southlake, Texas, produces a line of delightful dolls called Daddy's Long Legs. They seem to have excited quite a number of people in the doll world. We have received a large amount of mail asking about them and people telling us how thrilled they were about them. At this time, we have not seen any on the secondary market, but the 1990 dolls should be coming onto the market shortly. Some of these dolls are:

Boy Pig: Retired December 1990.

Indian (first edition): Retired December 1990 after one year.

Mimi: December 1990

Black Santa in tapestry: 1990. Approximately 25 white Santas were made.

Black Santa in velvet: 1990. Approximately 25 white Santas were made.

Boy and girl goat: Retired December 1991.

Raccoon: Retired June 1991.

Santa: black and white, 1991.

Uncle Sam: Retired December 1991.

Robby, Rose, and Rudy Rabbit: Retired December 1992.

Sofie: First black character to retire. December 1992.

Daphne: Retired December 1992.

Roxanne and Rachel Rabbit: Retired June 1992.

Lucky the Gambler: Retired December 1992.

James (groom) and Oliva (bride): Limited edition, 1992. Marriage license was available for each married couple purchased.

Limited edition Santa: Numbered and signed. 1992.

Choo-Choo: Retired September 1993.

Doc Moses: Retired September 1993.

Josie: Retired September 1993.

Nurse Garnet: Retired September 1993.

Faith: First Members edition doll. Exclusive to club members. 1993.

28" Santa from 1992 and 12" Faith, Daddy's Long Legs' first club doll. Daddy's Long Legs dolls are approximately $20.00 for the very small dolls. Most average between $65.00 and $145.00. *Courtesy Marie Ernst.*

29" BETTY THE BEAUTFIUL BRIDE by Deluxe Premium Corp., part of Deluxe Reading sold in grocery stores in 1957 to 1959. One-piece stuffed body and limbs with high heel feet. Doll with same style gown but with ruffles to waist was named ROSEMARY. She was a bridesmaid and the gown came in blue, yellow, or pink. Will be marked "AE" with a number such as 251. $85.00. *Courtesy Kathy Tvrdik.*

⤳ Disney ⤳

Disney collectibles and collectors have increased each and every year. In years gone by, collectors only wanted the old Disney collectibles. Today's collectors are happy with a few old items as well as newly issued collectibles. In recent years, Disney has hit the jackpot with collectibles associated with the release of new movies such as *Hook, The Little Mermaid, Beauty and the Beast,* and *Aladdin,* and the rescreening of the classic *Snow White.*

24" all cloth MICKEY AND MINNIE MOUSE with wire armatures for posing. No tags. Circa 1930s. 22" DOPEY with composition head and hands, stuffed cloth body. All original. Rare ventriloquist doll. 24" - $600.00 each; 22" - $485.00. *Courtesy Marian Jarmush.*

Adorable 12" SNEEZY in mint condition. Has cloth body with face mask, fake fur beard, and name printed on cap. All original. Original price tag: $1.50. From 1938. $245.00. *Courtesy Susan Giradot.*

All composition 12" DOC of the Seven Dwarfs. Velvet clothes, felt hat with name, and glasses. Original with arm tag. $425.00. *Courtesy Susan Giradot.*

8" PINOCCHIO made by Ideal Dolls. Wooden segmented body and limbs. Composition head with molded-on hat. Collar and tie are oil cloth and glued on. $265.00.

7½" GINGER in Disney's Davy Crockett Adventureland costume. All original including gun. From 1955. $100.00 up. *Courtesy Maureen Fukushima.*

GINGER as SAFARI GIRL from Disney's Adventureland Series of 1955. (There was also MOUSEKETEER GINGER VISITS MICKEY MOUSE CLUB of 1955. Has four outfits and all include a wonderful mask face of Mickey Mouse.) $100.00 up. *Courtesy Maureen Fukushima.*

7½" ORIENTAL PRINCESS from the 1955 Disney Adventureland Series using the GINGER doll. $100.00 up.
Courtesy Maureen Fukushima.

GINGER dressed as CINDERELLA from Fantasyland Series. Tiara is missing. From 1956. $100.00. *Courtesy Maureen Fukushima.*

7½" GINGER in Disney Fantasyland outfit of 1956. This one is the BLUE FAIRY. $100.00. *Courtesy Maureen Fukushima.*

8" GINGER with hard plastic body and vinyl head. From Disney's Tomorrowland Series. This one is SPACE PRINCESS. Others in the series are ROCKET PILOT, SUN PRINCESS, and SPACE GIRL. All have antennas. $125.00 up. *Courtesy Maureen Fukushima.*

12" all composition SNOW WHITE with molded hair and bow in front. Eyes are painted to side. One-piece body and head. This doll is now being attributed to Ideal by other doll authors, but she was most likely made for the dime store trade by another company. Clothes are not original. Doll unmarked and in very good condition. $150.00. *Courtesy Kathy Tvrdik.*

21" SNOW WHITE made by Sayco in 1950. All vinyl and original. Colors of clothes are called "crest colors" because they match the clothes of the original Disney's Snow White. Marked on head and right foot. $185.00 up. *Courtesy Jeannie Mauldin.*

SNOW WHITE made by Effanbee exclusively for Disneyland/Disneyworld. They also made SLEEPING BEAUTY, ALICE IN WONDERLAND, and CINDERELLA for the theme parks. $185.00. *Courtesy Sally Bethschieder.*

12" SNOW WHITE that was sold to the general public as part of Effanbee's Storybook Series. $85.00. *Courtesy Peggy Millhouse.*

15" SNOW WHITE was a premium doll offered in 1985 for one label from Final Touch fabric softner and $9.95. Vinyl head, cloth body and limbs. Painted features, painted-on red high heel shoes. Doll unmarked but dress tagged "Applause/Division of Wallace Berrie & Co., Inc. Woodland Hills, Ca 91367/Walt Disney Productions." Arm tagged "Piroette Dolls/ #3582 Snow White." $80.00. *Courtesy Genie Jinright.*

Regular edition of SNOW WHITE with large painted eyes and molded hair and ribbon. Made by Applause with Disney crest colors. $60.00. *Courtesy Roger Jones.*

16" crest color SNOW WHITE that could be purchased at Disney theme parks. Has rooted hair with cloth ribbon and inset eyes. $95.00. *Courtesy Roger Jones.*

10" Madame Alexander SNOW WHITE made in 1993. Wears the Disney crest colors. Limited edition. Made exclusively for Disneyland/Disneyworld. $150.00. *Courtesy Roger Jones.*

One of two SNOW WHITE dolls issued by The Franklin Mint. This one is a 14" porcelain doll dressed in the Disney crest colors. Wig is arranged with ribbon and bow. From 1993. $185.00. *Courtesy Peggy Millhouse.*

28" SNOW WHITE by Hildegarde Gunzel (Madame Alexander Co., Inc.) This was a special edition of 25 made for the Walt Disney Convention in 1992. Signed by Ms. Gunzel on cloth stomach. Price unknown. *Courtesy Pat Graff.*

14" SNOW WHITE from the "Land of Doom." Made by Lucky Bell for Woolworth in 1992. All vinyl with sleep eyes. $32.00. *Courtesy Pat Graff.*

8" SNOW WHITE made for Disney by Horsman, 1981–1983. Also made was CINDERELLA, ALICE IN WONDERLAND, and MARY POPPINS. $40.00. *Courtesy Pat Graff.*

12" Snow White by Royal House of Dolls. All vinyl with brown sleep eyes and rooted hair. From 1989. $75.00. *Courtesy Pat Graff.*

18½" all cloth Snow White with painted eyes, real eyelashes, and human hair wig. Made by Karin Heller of Germany in 1990. Limited edition of 125. $750.00. *Courtesy Pat Graff.*

11½" Evil Queen and Wicked Witch from Snow White story. Made by Bikin Express, Ltd. (Other characters may be seen in *Modern Collector Dolls, Sixth Series,* pages 67–69.) Each - $45.00. *Courtesy Pat Graff.*

8" Cinderella from Walt Disney Classics. Made by Horsman exclusively for Disneyland/Disneyworld in 1981. $46.00. *Courtesy Gloria Anderson.*

8" MOUSEKETEER made of plastic and vinyl with sleep eyes. Plastic cap is attached but clothes are removable. Marked "Horsman Doll, Inc. 1971." $30.00. *Courtesy Kathy Tvrdik.*

17" DANCING DONALD DUCK with cloth body, plastic head, and vinyl hands. Cap is missing. Marked "Walt Disney Productions." Made by Hasbro in Hong Kong. $60.00. *Courtesy Kathy Tvrdik.*

11" BELLE from Disney's *Beauty and the Beast.* Marked "Mattel. Licensed by Disney. 1991/Copyright W. Disney." $30.00. *Courtesy Kathy Tvrdik.*

THE BEAST from Disney's *Beauty and the Beast.* Removable mask and coat turns Beast into Prince. Made by Mattel in 1991. $30.00. *Courtesy Kathy Tvrdik.*

3½" MINNIE AND ME figures made of posable vinyl that could also be worn as hair barrettes. Left is MICKEY MOUSE and his playset accessories. Right is MINNIE MOUSE with a plug of bright pink hair. Dance accessories and removable skirt in playset. Below left is DAISY DUCK and her picnic set. She has a plug of yellow hair and removable skirt. Made by Mattel in China, 1990. Each - $12.00. *Courtesy Kathy Tvrdik.*

6" UNCLE SCROOGE made of plastic and vinyl with wire glasses. Has bendable arms and legs. Marked "1961 Walt Disney Productions" on tummy. $50.00. *Courtesy Kathy Tvrdik.*

⫷ Doll Artists ⫸
American and Foreign
See information about Doll Artists on pages 276–277.

Left: 5" Happy Hooligan. $25.00. Center: Delightful 2½" rendering of Howdy Doody and Hat. $35.00. Right: 2½" Santa from the Dolls My Mother Made Series. $30.00. All are hand sculptured and finished by Sara of Chaye's Shoppe in Queens, NY. *Courtesy Chaye "Sara" Arotsky.*

15½" Little Carmen of the American Classics Doll Collection from 1984. All vinyl with jointed waist. Tagged "Doll designed by Carole Bowling. Clothes designed by Connie Guardis, Miami, FL." Marked on head "13; A.M. Classic. 1984." $125.00. *Courtesy Pat Graff.*

16" porcelain Blossom with soft cloth body. Limited edition of 250. Made and designed by Yolanda Bello. All original. From 1988. $600.00. *Courtesy Pat Graff.*

15" LE BALLOON ROUGE is porcelain with soft cloth body. (Named for French children's movie from 1955.) Limited edition of 250. All original. Designed and made by Yolanda Bello. From 1989. $600.00. *Courtesy Pat Graff.*

14" HORSE SHOW in riding habit. Excellent quality. Designed by Yolanda Bello for Associated Dollmakers, Inc. in 1990. $125.00.

23" TIM made of maple wood with cloth body. Signed and numbered edition. All original. Made by Nancy Bruns of Brunswood Dolls. (Bruns later dolls are made of resin.) From 1986. Wood - $500.00 up; resin - $350.00 up. *Courtesy Pat Graff.*

21" porcelain ROSEMARY with soft cloth body. Original. Made by Madeline Neill-St. Clair of Canada in 1992. $1,000.00. *Courtesy Pat Graff.*

16" ANNIE HARMONY DOLL made of resin with soft cloth body and inset eyes. Limited edition of 450. Original by Edna Dali of Israel. From 1990. $800.00. *Courtesy Pat Graff.*

20" porcelain LIZABETH ANN with soft cloth body. Has inset eyes and holes in feet for stand. Designed by Dianne Effner in 1990 for Collectables. Limited to 1,000. Signed by Pheples Parkins. $450.00. *Courtesy Pat Graff.*

16" ROSALEA from 1989. Designed by Margaret Jones for Alresford of England. $285.00. *Courtesy Pat Graff.*

16½" COLIN made in France by C&R Club, now known as Corolle. Original. From 1979. $80.00. *Courtesy Pat Graff.*

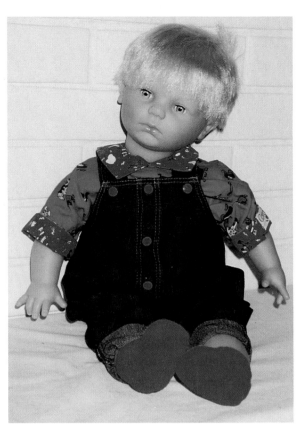

19" Emmy and 21" Florian made of vinyl with soft cloth bodies. Both were made in France by Corolle. She was made in 1990 and he in 1989. Both are original. 19" - $160.00; 21" - $175.00. *Courtesy Pat Graff.*

22" Lola and Marie, standing, and Manon, sitting, made of vinyl with soft cloth bodies. All original. Dolls were designed by Malou Ancelin for Corolle of France in 1987. Each - $275.00. *Courtesy Pat Graff.*

21" DOROTHEE made of resin with soft cloth body and enameled eyes. Limited edition of 100. Made in France for Joelle Le Mason. Signed "Heloise" as designer. $1,200.00. *Courtesy Pat Graff.*

22" WILLI & LILLI made of vinyl with soft body and legs. Second edition had vinyl legs. Original. Marked with turtle mark and "Schildkrot." Made in Germany, 1984–1985. Each - $125.00. *Courtesy Pat Graff.*

18" SLEEPING BEAUTY using the HANNERL doll. Vinyl with jointed waist. Original. Marked with turtle mark and "Schildkrot." Made in Germany in 1985. $70.00. *Courtesy Pat Graff.*

17" vinyl KATRINA with soft cloth body. All original. Made in Germany for Engle-Puppen, 1988. $145.00. *Courtesy Pat Graff.*

23" BINCHEN II from the 1989 first series limited edition of 500. (1990 edition was 1,500.) All original. Made by Sigikid-Sabine Esche of Germany. $700.00.
Courtesy Pat Graff.

23" GILBERT II made of vinyl with soft cloth body. All original. Limited edition of 750. Designed by Gabriele Braun for Sigikid of Germany. $775.00. *Courtesy Pat Graff.*

26" FLORENTINA designed by Ilsa Wippler for Sigikid in 1994. Vinyl with soft cloth body, painted eyes, and human hair wig. Limited edition of 500. $700.00.
Courtesy Pat Graff.

17" SAILOR BOY made of all cloth with button eyes. All original. Made in Germany by Stupsi. $95.00.
Courtesy Pat Graff.

21" GLENA made of vinyl with soft cloth body. All original. Designed and made by Suzanne Gibson in 1984. $100.00. *Courtesy Pat Graff.*

12" ALICE made and designed by Suzanne Gibson in 1986. All vinyl and original. Her animal friends are made by Steiff. $350.00. *Courtesy Pat Graff.*

20" all vinyl MOPPET with open mouth and two lower teeth. All original. Made by Good-Kruger in 1991. Limited edition of 1,500. $200.00. *Courtesy Pat Graff.*

22" all vinyl ANNIE ROSE made by Good-Kruger in 1990. All original. Limited edition of 1,000. $325.00. *Courtesy Pat Graff.*

18½" vinyl and cloth unnamed doll made special for Spiegel. Made in Germany by Gotz. Has TRIXIE face with sleep eyes and lashes. **$90.00.** *Courtesy Pat Graff.*

18½" JELLYBEAN from Sweet Inspirations Series by Gorham in 1985. All cloth with button eyes. All original. **$35.00.** *Courtesy Pat Graff.*

11" ROSE of the Valentine Ladies Series made by Gorham in 1989. All porcelain and original. Limited edition of 2,500. **$250.00.** *Courtesy Pat Graff.*

20" EMMANUEL designed by Sylvia Natterer as one of her Fanouch and Friends Dolls. All vinyl and original. Made for Gotz of Germany in 1990. **$250.00.** *Courtesy Pat Graff.*

25½" FLEURETTE made by Gotz of Germany and designed by Sylvia Natterer in 1991. Vinyl with soft cloth body. All original. $425.00. *Courtesy Pat Graff.*

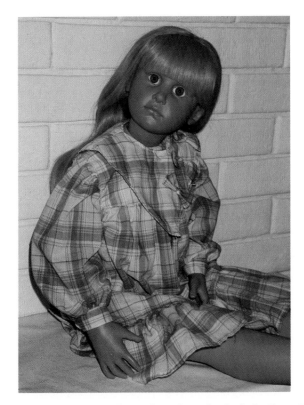

28" MURIEL made of vinyl with soft cloth body. All original. Winner of "Dolls" Award and designed by Hildegarde Gunzel from the Classic Children Series of 1989. $350.00. *Courtesy Pat Graff.*

28" HORST made of vinyl with soft cloth body. All original. Designed by Hildegarde Gunzel. From the Classic Children Series of 1989. $350.00. *Courtesy Pat Graff.*

20" INGRID & JAN made of vinyl with soft cloth bodies. Designed and made by Sonja Hartman from 1986 to 1988. Both are all original. Each - $425.00. *Courtesy Pat Graff.*

13" POLLY designed by Sarah Kaye and made by Anri of Italy in 1990. Maple wooden doll with jointed knees and elbows. Limited edition of 1,000. All original. $600.00. *Courtesy Pat Graff.*

17" unknown character with pronounced Roman nose. Possibly represents a celebrity or character. All vinyl with jointed waist. All original. Made by and marked "Famosa." Circa 1978. $95.00. *Courtesy Pat Graff.*

14" all vinyl INDIAN BOY made by Furga of Italy in 1992. Original. $50.00. *Courtesy Pat Graff.*

21" porcelain SCARLETT with soft cloth body. Made by Gambini of Italy in 1989. All original. Limited edition of 1,500. $225.00. *Courtesy Pat Graff.*

8½" MAGGIE designed by Helen Kish for the Dakin Elegante Series in 1985. All vinyl and original. $75.00. *Courtesy Pat Graff.*

Cute 10" all vinyl dolls made and designed by Helen Kish in 1984. Each - $85.00. *Courtesy Marie Ernst.*

HANNAH portraying FROLIC, Amish for a working party of friends and neighbors coming together to raise a barn, to make a quilt, or to harvest. Limited to 500. Made in 1991. $675.00 up. *Courtesy Lawton Doll Co.*

NDEKO represents an older sister carrying her baby sister. From the Cherished Customs Collection by Wendy Lawton. Limited edition of 500. From 1991. $900.00 up. *Courtesy Lawton Doll Co.*

19" SWEET CHEEKS DOLLS made of all cloth. The boy is COCOA BUTTER; the girl is VANILLA. Both are all original. Made by Lloyderson in 1985. Each - $50.00.
Courtesy Pat Graff.

12" porcelain ABBY with extra joints at knees, ankles, and elbows. #29 of a limited edition of 50. Alice Lester is the designer and this is the first doll from her first series. Has trunk, wardrobe, and accessories. From 1990. $1,300.00. *Courtesy Pat Graff.*

24" MARA made of porcelain with soft cloth body. Limited edition of 150. All original. Designed and made by Janet Ness in 1991. $900.00. *Courtesy Pat Graff.*

20" SINCERITY made by Lee Middleton in 1988. Vinyl with soft cloth body. Has very character face. $200.00. *Courtesy Pat Graff.*

18" BRIDE with porcelain head and limbs. Soft cloth body. All original. Limited edition of 2,000. Made by Dolls by Pauline in 1989. $225.00. *Courtesy Pat Graff.*

17" porcelain ESKIMO GIRL with soft cloth body. All original. Limited edition of 3,000. Made by Dolls by Pauline in 1990. $225.00. *Courtesy Pat Graff.*

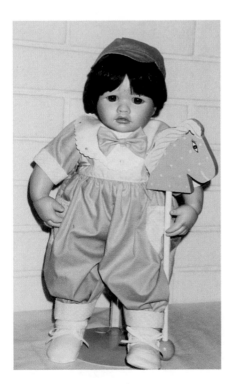

17" ALEXANDER with porcelain head and limbs. Soft cloth body. All original. Made by Dolls by Pauline in 1990. $225.00. *Courtesy Pat Graff.*

17½" vinyl PETRA with soft cloth body. All original. Designed by Eva Reick in 1988 for Gustel Weid. $95.00. *Courtesy Pat Graff.*

21" FRANZI made of vinyl with soft cloth body. All original. Designed by Eva Reick for Gustel Weid in 1991. $145.00. *Courtesy Pat Graff.*

18" vinyl RENEE with soft cloth body. All original. Made by Tiffany in 1986. Clothes are tagged "Gotz." $130.00. *Courtesy Pat Graff.*

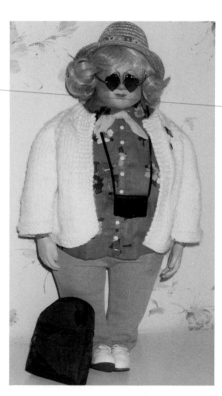

20" TOURIST was made by Amazing Grace in 1988. Made of porcelain with soft cloth body. This delightful character is signed "Ronfee Apr. '88." Limited edition of 250. All original. $350.00. *Courtesy Pat Graff.*

16" LINDA LEE, model #5/85/2304. Has vinyl head and lower arms with the rest being cloth. Made in 1985 by Rothkirch. All original. $300.00. *Courtesy Pat Graff.*

14" NICOLETTE is vinyl with a soft cloth body. Made in 1993 by Rothkirch. Limited edition of 500. All original. $300.00. *Courtesy Pat Graff.*

21" CHELSEA made of vinyl with soft cloth body. All original. Made in 1988 by Royal House of Dolls. $180.00. *Courtesy Pat Graff.*

28" vinyl MARTINA with soft cloth body. All original. Made in 1989–1990 by Gadco. Designed by Rotraut Schrott. (Gadco made a reduced size of this doll and also an overproduced porcelain edition.) Old Schoenhut piano was made prior to 1935. $425.00. *Courtesy Pat Graff.*

11½" porcelain ALEXANDER, a Metropolitan Museum of Art doll dressed in 1890s costume. All original. Made by Shackman in 1984. $60.00. *Courtesy Pat Graff.*

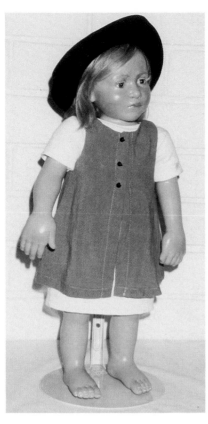

16" CHARLOTTE is a wax over porcelain doll with cloth body. Made and designed by Nerissa Shaub in 1990. Signed artist proof. $1,200.00. *Courtesy Pat Graff.*

12" KIKOSITO made of vinyl with soft cloth body. All original and came in a carrying bag. Made in 1988 by VIR in Spain. $35.00. *Courtesy Pat Graff.*

17" HANAKO made in 1982 by Berjusa of Spain. All vinyl sexed girl. All original. $60.00. *Courtesy Pat Graff.*

20" FOFY made in 1986 by Berjusa of Spain. Vinyl with soft cloth body. All original. $60.00. *Courtesy Pat Graff.*

16" POUTY PUSS made of vinyl with soft cloth body. All original. Made in 1984 by Berjusa of Spain. $55.00. *Courtesy Pat Graff.*

13" all vinyl MICKEY designed and made by Marg Spangler in 1979. Original. $60.00. *Courtesy Pat Graff.*

18½" LITTLE BEAR & MORNING STAR are Navajo children made of all vinyl. Part of the Starshine Dolls of 1990. Made by Gotz of Germany. $225.00. *Courtesy Pat Graff.*

19½" MARY HAD A LITTLE LAMB made of vinyl with cloth body. Made by Steiff in 1990. Limited edition of 1,000. All original. $825.00. *Courtesy Pat Graff.*

15" hand-carved wooden doll with jointed elbows and knees. Glass googly eyes and lashes. If you cover half of face, she appears to be smiling. Cover the other half and she is frowning. Marked "FT" and "'76" on bottom of foot. Carved on boots. Made in 1976. $450.00. *Courtesy Pat Graff.*

27" CAMILLA with porcelain head and limbs and soft cloth body. All original. Limited edition of 150. First original sculpture by artist Charlene Thanos. $1,350.00. *Courtesy Pat Graff.*

28" JOCELYN dolls made of porcelain and cloth. Designed and made by Charlene Thanos. Originally meant to be a limited edition of 250, but ended up being 100 blondes in blue coats with pink piping and pink dresses. There are 50 with red hair and green eyes. Their coats are seafoam green with purple piping. These dolls are far more beautiful than shown. Each - $1,300.00. *Courtesy Charlene Thanos.*

36" porcelain and cloth GISELLE was designed by Charlene Thanos. The quality of the clothing is unsurpassed. A truly beautiful doll. $2,500.00. *Courtesy Charlene Thanos.*

28–33" AMBER LAUREN is another beauty from the hands of Charlene Thanos. Limited edition of 50. Made in 1994. (This wonderful child also is made with brown eyes and medium brown hair and dressed in moss rose with rose trim. The matching bonnet has moss rose flowers.) $1,700.00. *Courtesy Charlene Thanos.*

This 36" doll is named ENCHANTRESS and there is no better name to describe her. Created by Charlene Thanos. $4,800.00 up. *Courtesy Charlene Thanos.*

13" porcelain AMANDA MARIE designed by Robert Tonner in 1992. Signed limited edition of 50. Painted eyes, mohair wig. Attention to clothing is outstanding. $650.00. *Courtesy Pat Graff.*

17½" doll made by Wernicke (formally Koenig & Wernicke – K&W) of Germany in 1984. Rigid vinyl with soft cloth body. Crier box in body. Limited edition of 1,000. $165.00. *Courtesy Pat Graff.*

16" LILY FLOWER SELLER designed by Faith Wick. Made by Dakin as part of the Elegante Series in 1984. Vinyl with soft cloth body. All original. $150.00. *Courtesy Pat Graff.*

27" KRISTIE made of vinyl with soft cloth body. Head designed by Judith Turner. Made by Royal House of Dolls in 1986. All original. $200.00. *Courtesy Pat Graff.*

16" ASHLEY designed by Susan Wakeen in 1989. Vinyl and cloth. Inset glass eyes with lashes. Limited to 2,500. $175.00. *Courtesy Pat Graff.*

Domec Toy Co.

Domec Toy Co. was in business from 1918 through the 1930s. Although they merged with Century Doll Co., they retained the Domec trademark. They manufactured the majority of the carnival dolls and speciality items for the Atlantic City Boardwalk, Coney Island, and many state fairs. Domec made a Patsy look-alike marked "Kewty" in 1930.

Right: 24" marked "Domec N.Y." Has sleep eyes, celluloid teeth, and molded tongue. Composition shoulder head with jointed legs. Upper body and arms replaced. Arms may have been jointed at elbows. $275.00 up. *Courtesy Virginia Sofie.*

14" KEWTY is a PATSY look-alike with tin sleep eyes. Right arm molded bent at elbow. Made by Domec Toy Co. in 1930 and marked on body. $365.00.
Courtesy Glorya Woods.

7½" dolls like this one were made by companies such as Dutchess, Moulded Arts, Nay-Mare, Elite, A&H, and Princess Grace. They had stapled-on clothes and mohair wigs. Can have painted or sleep eyes. They were in Wards and Sears catalogs throughout the early 1950s and were in most dime stores. Value is small unless doll is a personality. $4.00.

8" all hard plastic RANDI made by Dutchess Dolls. This is another doll made from the Cosmopolitan GINGER mold. Since RANDI was a purchased blank (nude) doll and only dressed by Dutchess, she is hard to identify unless found in original box. In box - $55.00. *Courtesy Maureen Fukushima.*

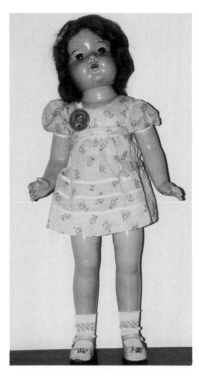

22" MISS CHARMING made by Eegee in 1936. All composition with sleep eyes, open mouth, and mohair wig. Original clothes, added pin. $475.00. *Courtesy Gloria Anderson.*

12" SHELLY made of plastic and vinyl with grow hair feature, painted eyes, and original clothes. She was a copy of TAMMY made by Ideal. Marked "Eegee" on head. $20.00. *Courtesy Kathy Tvrdik.*

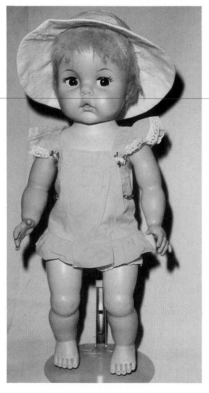

17" SNIFFLES made of plastic and vinyl with rooted hair and painted eyes. Marked "#7" and near top of head "Eegee/18 U-2." Original. $20.00. *Courtesy Kathy Tvrdik.*

14" SOFTINA from 1967. (Sold also as BOOTSIE in 1966.) One-piece body and limbs. Made of plastic and vinyl. Painted eyes. Open mouth nurser. Came with or without wig. Marked "Eegee/16VS" on head. $12.00. *Courtesy Kathy Tvrdik.*

11½" and 12" DOLLY PARTON dolls made of plastic and vinyl. Bendable knees and jointed waist. Marked "Dolly Parton/Eegee Co./Hong Kong" on head and "Goldberger Mfg. Co., 1980" on box. Each - $30.00. *Courtesy David Spurgeon.*

Left: 10" COMBAT SOLDIER made of plastic and vinyl. Molded hair and painted features. One-piece jumpsuit with velcro fastner. "Eegee/H-18" if marked, but most will only have "Made in China." $10.00. *Courtesy Don Tvrdik.*

Effanbee

All doll companies have certain dolls that seem to be more desirable to the collectors than others. With Effanbee, the Patsy family is foremost and rivals the other most popular doll, Shirley Temple. In the more modern era, the dolls most sought after are the Effanbee Club dolls and the Legend Series.

Effanbee has produced a vast amount of high quality dolls in the plastic and vinyl era. They should be much more collectible than they are, especially the lady dolls from the Grande Dames Series and Seasons Series. The Internationals/Storybook dolls will most likely remain about the same. The same can be said

about all doll companies that produced this style doll. The present thinking is if you like the Effanbees made in recent years, it is a good time to buy. The cost is not out of reach yet, particularly on sets mentioned as well as the Jan Hargara, Faith Wick, Edna Hibel, and Joyce Stafford designed dolls.

EFFANBEE LIMITED EDITION CLUB DOLLS

The first doll was a standard doll taken from the marketing line and redressed in a fantastic outfit/pillow. She is a rare and beautiful doll, but her 25" size makes her large enough to pass up. Effanbee had the concept of the Limited Edition Club, but they had no mailing list. Mr. Leroy Fadem, co-owner of Effanbee, flew to Independence, Missouri, to visit with Kim McKim of Kimport Dolls. Mr. Fadem asked Kimport to do the actual mailing of the flyers that introduced the doll. This author was working at Kimport Dolls when this took place and the prospect of Effanbee's success in this venture was bleak to our owner and the staff. Almost all of the doll business was in antique dolls at the time. The ratio of dolls sold to flyers sent out was 1 to 10 and that surprised all of us.

LIMITED EDITION CLUB DOLLS

	Production Year	Number Made
Precious Baby	1975	872
Patsy	1976	1,200
Dewees Cochran	1977	3,166
Crowning Glory	1978	2,200
Skippy	1979	3,485
Susan B. Anthony	1980	3,485
Renoir Girl/watering can	1981	3,835
Princess Diana	1982	4,220
Sherlock Holmes	1983	4,470
Bubbles	1984	4,470
Goya's Don Manuel	1985	4,470
China head doll	1986	4,470
Baby Grumpy (porcelain)	1987	2,500
Baby Grumpy (vinyl)	1987	5,000

THE LEGENDS SERIES

	Production Year
W.C. Fields	1980
John Wayne (cowboy)	1981
John Wayne (soldier)	1982
Mae West	1983
Groucho Marx	1983
Judy Garland as Dorothy	1984
Lucille Ball	1985
Liberace (Mr. Showman)	1986
James Cagney	1987
Humphrey Bogart	1989
Claudette Colbert	1990

PRESIDENTS SERIES

	Production Year
Theodore Roosevelt	1984
Franklin Delano Roosevelt	1985
John Fitzgerald Kennedy	1986
Dwight D. Eisenhower	1987
Harry S. Truman	1988
Thomas Jefferson	1989
Andrew Jackson	1990

GREAT MOMENTS IN MUSIC

Louis Armstrong	1984

GREAT MOMENTS IN HISTORY

Winston Churchill	1984
Eleanor Roosevelt	1985

GREAT MOMENTS IN SPORTS

Babe Ruth	1985
Muhammad Ali	1986

WORLD'S GREATEST HEROS

General Douglas McArthur	1991

GREAT MOMENTS IN TELEVISION

Art Carney (Ed Norton)	1986
Jackie Gleason (Ralph Kramden)	1986

NEW WORLD COLLECTION

Queen Isabella	1990
Christopher Columbus	1990

Center: 18" BUBBLES toddler. Right: 16" BUBBLES in original outfit. Left: 18" BABY DIMPLES by Horsman that is original but missing coat. All have tin sleep eyes and cloth bodies. 18" BUBBLES - $325.00; 16" - $275.00; 18" DIMPLES - $300.00. *Courtesy Turn of Century Antiques.*

15" doll from 1920s and marked "Effanbee/Baby Dainty" on composition shoulder plate. Arms and legs are also composition. Stuffed cloth body and upper legs. Molded hair and painted features. Disc jointed arms. $265.00. *Courtesy June Schultz.*

Right: A wonderful all cloth doll with oil-painted features. Cloth body with material on back of head and skirt matching. Has original Effanbee heart pin and tag. Circa 1943. $475.00.
Below: Tagged "N.R.A." with American eagle and "Effanbee." N.R.A. stands for National Recovery Administration which was established during the Great Depression of 1930s. *Courtesy Kris Lundquist.*

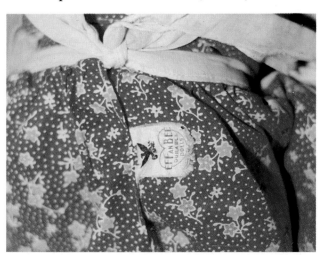

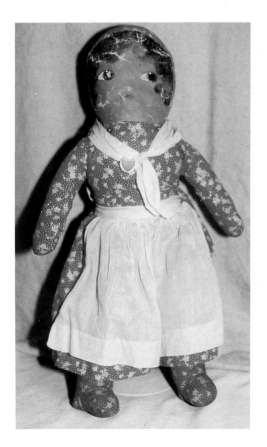

19" ROSEMARY with composition shoulderhead, arms, and legs. Stuffed cloth body. Tin sleep eyes. Open mouth with four teeth. Original wig and clothes with replaced shoes and socks. From 1925. $385.00. *Courtesy Jeannie Mauldin.*

18" LAMKINS made of all composition and is fully jointed. Has sleep eyes, painted hair, small open mouth, and gold ring molded and painted on curled left finger. All fingers on right hand curled. $500.00. *Courtesy Jeannie Mauldin.*

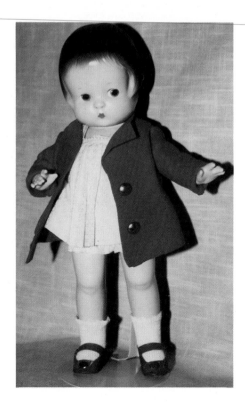

14" PATSY made of all composition with molded, painted hair and painted features. Marked on back. All original except missing red felt hat to match coat. Below is a close-up of tag on dress. $365.00. *Courtesy Susan Giradot.*

14" PATSY with painted eyes and hair. Original felt coat and tam. Also has original metal heart bracelet. **$365.00 up.** *Courtesy Gloria Anderson.*

14" PATSY is all original with original box. Wearing Patsy Doll Club pin. Has metal heart bracelet. With box and pin - **$450.00 up.** *Courtesy Gloria Anderson.*

11" PATSY JR. is in mint condition and all original. Has metal heart wrist tag and Patsy Doll Club pin. **$285.00.** *Courtesy Gloria Anderson.*

9" PATSYETTE with wardrobe of outfits made from 1930s patterns by owner, Glorya Woods. Redressed - **$225.00;** trunk/wardrobe - **$485.00.**

19" PATSY ANN dressed in original organdy dress. Shoes and socks replaced. Has sleep eyes and lashes. A 1929 Christmas gift with trunk filled with dresses made from McCall patterns. $485.00 *Courtesy Virgina Sofie.*

19" all composition doll with green sleep eyes. Marked "Effanbee/Patsy Ann/Pat. 1283558." Dress made in 1930 from McCall Patsy Ann pattern. Redressed - $425.00 up. *Courtesy Virginia Sofie.*

22" composition PATSY LOU with wig and sleep eyes. All original. $485.00. *Courtesy Glorya Woods.*

30" PATSY MAE is the largest in the PATSY family. Sleep eyes and human hair wig. She holds PATSY BABY that has sleep eyes. Both are original. PATSY MAE - $785.00; PATSY BABY - $285.00. *Courtesy Glorya Woods.*

14" PATRICIA made of composition with human hair wig and sleep eyes. Original and in mint condition. $385.00. *Courtesy Glorya Woods.*

14" first ANNE SHIRLEY using the PATRICIA doll. Human hair wig with full bangs and braided pigtails. Original. $400.00. *Courtesy Glorya Woods.*

Back: 14" BLACK PATSY with molded painted hair as well as three tuffs of braided hair. Doll is marked "Effanbee/ Patsy/Pat. Pend./Doll." Front: The all composition dolls range from 7¼" to 9" and are unmarked. The dolls with three tuffs of hair were sold as TOPSY. Later in the 1930s, the babies were sold as AMOSANDRA from radio's "Amos and Andy Show." 14" - $500.00; 7¼" - $65.00; 9" - $85.00. *Courtesy Virginia Sofie.*

8" composition TINYETTE is a fully jointed toddler with molded hair and painted features. Clothes are original but may be missing tam. Marked "Effanbee" on head and body. Body is also marked "Baby Tinyette." $265.00. *Courtesy Shirley Merrill.*

AMERICAN CHILDREN designed by Dewees Cochron. Doll on left is 21" tall with sleep eyes and human hair wig. Both are original and marked "Effanbee/ American Children" on heads and "Anne Shirley" on back. Each - $1,100.00 up. *Courtesy Frasher Doll Auctions.*

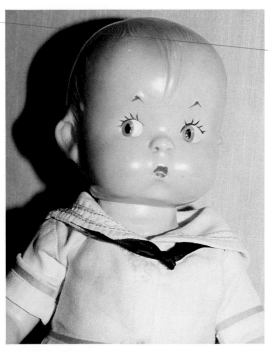

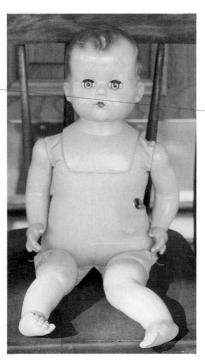

14" SKIPPY made of all compostion with molded, painted hair and eyes. All original. Marked "Patsy" on torso. $450.00. *Courtesy Susan Giradot.*

20" HEART BEAT BABY has a key wound mechanism in torso. Cloth and composition with glassene sleep eyes and hair lashes. Circa 1948. $145.00. *Courtesy Kay Bransky.*

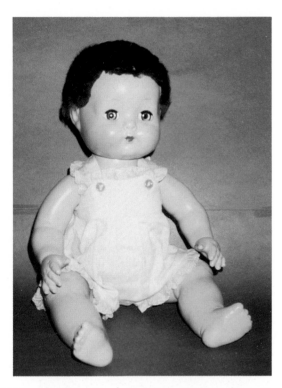

18" SWEETIE PIE, MICKEY, or BABY BRIGHT EYES. Same doll used for all three and unless in box or with tags, it is unknown which one it is. Made of composition with sleep eyes, lashes, and caracul wig. Can have flirty eyes. $35.00. *Courtesy Ellyn McCorkell.*

All original 22" BRIGHT EYES from1946 or 1947. Composition with glassene flirty sleep eyes and caracul wig. $400.00. *Courtesy Ellyn McCorkell.*

27" LITTLE LADY of 1945. All composition with cotton string wig, sleep eyes, and latex arms with individual fingers for gloves. $600.00. *Courtesy Virgina Sofie.*

27" LITTLE LADY made of all composition with sleep eyes and latex arms. All original in bridal outfit. Doll is unmarked in this size. $600.00. *Courtesy Susan Giridot.*

21" marked ANNE SHIRLEY with sleep eyes, human hair wig, and all original including metal heart bracelet. Made of composition with latex arms. **$500.00.** *Courtesy Susan Giradot.*

21" all composition LITTLE LADY from 1947. Brown glassene eyes and wonderful wig. Original. **$500.00.** *Courtesy Patricia A. Wood.*

21" all composition LITTLE LADY dressed in all original ballgown. Hair in original set. Marked on back "Ann Shirley." **$500.00.** *Courtesy Jeannie Nespoli.*

21" all composition HONEY from 1948–1949. Has human hair wig. Original except bow and necklace. **$450.00.** *Courtesy Gloria Anderson.*

18" LITTLE LADY as ALICE IN WONDERLAND from 1946. All composition with sleep eyes and yarn hair. Bracelet added. $450.00. *Courtesy Jeannie Nespoli.*

13" all composition CANDY KID toddlers. Both are original except missing shoes and socks. Left doll is in 1946 Wards catalog with suitcase and extra clothes. Both marked "Effanbee" on head and back. Childhood dolls of Shirley Merrill. Each - $250.00.

19" all hard plastic HONEY WALKER with sleep eyes and closed mouth. All original. Marked "Effanbee" on both head and body. $400.00. *Courtesy June Schultz.*

17" HONEY as designer doll FASHION MISS from 1956. Jointed ankles allow feet to be flat or high heeled or positioned like a ballerina. Sleep eyes and glued-on wig. $375.00. *Courtesy Jeannie Nespoli.*

24" CUDDLE UP from 1954. Vinyl head and limbs, oil cloth body. Has deeply molded hair, sleep eyes, and open/closed mouth with two lower teeth. All original with original box. With box - $145.00. *Courtesy Jeannie Mauldin.*

11" all vinyl MICKEY FOOTBALL has molded-on helmet and original clothes. Replaced shoes. $85.00. *Courtesy Kathy Tvrdik.*

18" BETTINA made of plastic and vinyl. Has sleep eyes and rooted hair. Marked "Effanbee 1961" on head but this doll and outfit is shown in the 1985 catalog. All original. $100.00. *Courtesy Jeannie Mauldin.*

14" all vinyl doll with character face. Doll is 1962 SUZETTE and she was marketed in Blue Bird and Girl Scout uniforms. Missing white socks and black shoes. Marked "Effanbee" on head. $125.00.

11" LADY ASCOT from the Grande Dame Series of 1981. Limited to 125 black dolls. Has certificate and number. $75.00. *Courtesy Hazel Adams.*

15" RUBY from the Grande Dame Series of 1980. All original. Came in black and white version. $75.00. *Courtesy Hazel Adams.*

11" MISS BLACK AMERICA dolls made from 1977 to 1979. Head will be marked 1975. Note costume variations. If the material ran out, it was replaced but not always with the same design. Each - $30.00. *Left courtesy Renie Culp; right courtesy Hazel Adams.*

11" POCOHONTAS from 1977–1978. Will be marked "Effanbee 1975/1476" on head. $30.00. *Courtesy Renie Culp.*

11" DAVY CROCKETT from the Historical Collection of 1977–1978. Doll will be marked 1975. $30.00. *Courtesy Sally Bethscheider.*

11" HALF PINT dolls from the Crochet Classics of 1976. Doll will be marked "Effanbee/1966" on head and "Effanbee/2400" on back. Each - $45.00. *Courtesy Renie Culp.*

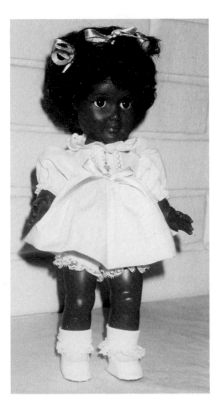

11" SISSY from the One World Collection made by Effanbee in 1983. Vinyl with sleep eyes and lashes. $45.00. *Courtesy Pat Graff.*

17" BILLY BUM made of plastic and vinyl with sleep eyes and rooted hair. Marked "Effanbee 1979/Faith Wick" on head. Tagged "Faith Wick Originals/Billy Bum." $75.00. *Courtesy Genie Jinright.*

Left: 16" CLOWN marketed from 1980 to 1981. Right: 16" GIRL CLOWN marketed from 1980 to 1983. Both were designed by Faith Wick for Effanbee. Head marked "Effanbee/1979/Faith Wick." Tagged "Faith Wick Originals." Each - $65.00. *Courtesy Renie Culp.*

18" LADY ANGELIQUE designed by Eugenia Dukas in 1988. Limited edition of 750. Made for Effanbee to market. Porcelain with soft cloth body and gray painted eyes. $175.00. *Courtesy Pat Graff.*

18" ROYAL BRIDE – DIANA, PRINCESS OF WALES. All vinyl with painted eyes. Dressed in copy of actual wedding gown. Has yard long train on gown. Part of the Limited Edition Effanbee Club dolls in 1982. $100.00. *Courtesy Kathy Tvrdik.*

8" LIL INNOCENTS also called LIL SWEETHEARTS. Made in 1980s and had a variety of costumes. $40.00.

21" RACHAEL made of vinyl with soft cloth body. Limited edition of 1,500. Made by Effanbee in 1989. $85.00 up. *Courtesy Pat Graff.*

8" all hard plastic VICKI BALLERINA with round body. Has sleep eyes with molded lashes. Excellent details on feet with dimples above toes. Doll is unmarked. Marketed and distributed by Elite. In box - $65.00. *Courtesy Maureen Fukushima.*

8" VICKI dressed as one of Elite's characters named RUTH. Original. In box - $65.00. *Courtesy Maureen Fukushima.*

8" VICKI with jointed knees and wide spread legs. Appears as she was purchased with outfit #V-607. (If outfit was purchased separately it was #V-407.) Doll has saran wig. From mid-1950s. In box - $65.00. *Courtesy Maureen Fukushima.*

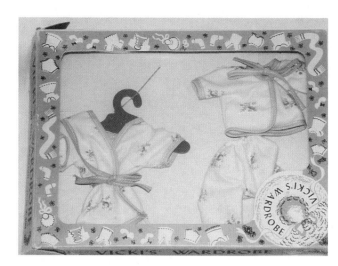

Left: One style of window box that extra outfits for VICKI came in. This one is V-614 "Dutch." Right: Another style of window box made for VICKI wardrobe. Each - $8.00–10.00. *Courtesy Maureen Fukushima.*

Above: 8" VICKI LEE was sold with just panties and her box is marked "Dress me. Undress me." Has mohair wig. She was first marketed in 1953. $65.00. *Courtesy Maureen Fukushima.*

Left: This is another VICKI LEE that is original in box. $65.00. *Courtesy Maureen Fukushima.*

15" "dress me" doll made of plastic and vinyl with sleep eyes/lashes and painted mustache. Marked "Fiber-Craft/Materials Corp./1988/Made in China." $25.00. *Courtesy Kathy Tvrdik.*

8" all composition doll jointed at shoulders only. Eyes are painted to side. Painted-on ribbed socks and shoes. Mohair wig. All original in box. Marked on back "Reliable/Made/in/Canada." From mid 1930s. $85.00 up. *Courtesy Phyllis Kates.*

15½" vinyl doll made in Belguim by Unica in the mid 1960s. Clothes are original. Her eyes are unique. Instead of blue eyes, common for blonde European dolls, hers are brown. $45.00. *Courtesy Pat Graff.*

10" all plastic RODDY WALKING PRINCESS has sleep eyes, open mouth, and both thumbs modeled up. Neck on these dolls are tall so head can be wobbly. All original. Mint condition - $85.00. *Courtesy Gloria Anderson.*

15" all hard plastic PAULIE has open/closed mouth with two painted upper teeth. Head turns as she walks. Marked "Rosebud/Made in England/Pat. No. 667901" on back and "Rosebud" on head. $60.00.
Courtesy Kathy Tvrdik.

16" ROSEBUD BABY has vinyl head and limbs with cloth body. Has squeaker in head. Eyes painted to side. Original clothes. Marked "Rosebud." Circa 1959. $70.00. *Courtesy Kathy Tvrdik.*

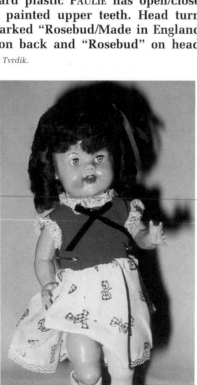

12" all hard plastic ROSEBUD with open mouth, two upper teeth, and sleep eyes. All fingers are separated. Has jointed knees. $45.00. *Courtesy Kathy Tvrdik.*

12" HELGA made of very light plastic combined with celluloid residue. Incised on neck "1956" with turtle mark. All original. $90.00. *Courtesy Pat Graff.*

Very collectible 1940s HULA GIRL made of composition style material. Swings from side to side on a spring. Souvenir doll from Hawaii. Original. $85.00 up. *Courtesy Patricia Wood.*

10" HAWAIIAN made of stockinette. Has yarn hair. Attached to wooden base. Original and in excellent condition. Pre-World War II. $15.00.

19" all hard plastic doll marked DIANA with diamond below name. The mark is on head and body. Glued on wig, flirty eyes, and swivel waist. Original. $100.00. *Courtesy Marian Alessi.*

Adorable 9" MARA BETH made of hard plastic. Has sleep eyes with hair lashes. Mohair wig. All original. Marked "Furga/Italy/17" on head. From 1954. Rare in this size. $125.00.

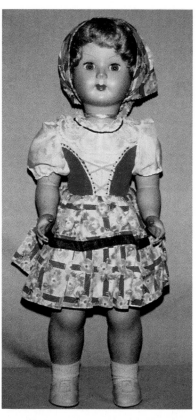

27" Italian doll used as bed doll or to sit on a chair. Also used as child's play doll. Made from early 1950s to 1960. Has large cryer box in stomach or back. Sleep eyes and lashes. This doll mold was used by several companies including Ava, Bella, Cares, and Bonomi. Purchased as blank then dressed and marketed by one of these companies. $185.00. *Courtesy Kathy Tvrdik.*

26" walker made of early plastic and cellulite. Has sleep eyes and large cryer box in stomach. Head turns from side to side when walking. All original. Marked "Made in Italy/Cares" on head with "Cares/Brev. 4912200" on back. $195.00. *Courtesy Carol Wetheria.*

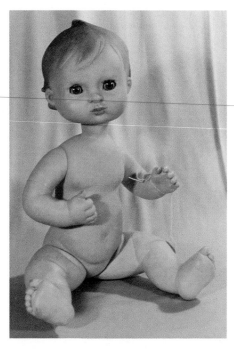

17" character baby made by Furga. All vinyl with spray painted hair, tiny ears, and sleep eyes. Marked from ear to ear on back of head "Furga, Italy." Also marked "Furga" on inside left thigh and upper right arm. $65.00. *Courtesy Marie Ernst.*

9" Lenci type doll with oil-painted mask face and cloth covered wire armature for posing. Made in early 1930s in Sicily. $55.00. *Courtesy Pat Graff.*

10" doll made in late 1940s in Occupied Japan. Painted bisque with molded hair and painted features. Jointed at shoulders and hips. Molded, painted-on shoes and socks. Wearing cotton dress. Original box calls her PAM. In box - $75.00. *Courtesy Susan Giradot.*

Very unusual 9" Mexican dolls. Wrist tags are marked "Ideal Doll Co." so it can be assumed that American companies made these souvenir dolls for Mexico. The wrist tags are gold foil and much like the NANCY ANN style wrist tag. Can be seen on girl's arm. Each - $65.00. *Courtesy Patricia Wood.*

6½–9" all composition souvenir dolls from Mexico. Boy on far right made by Ideal Doll Co. for Mexico. Others may have been made by Ideal or another American company. All are original. Each - $65.00. *Courtesy David Spurgeon.*

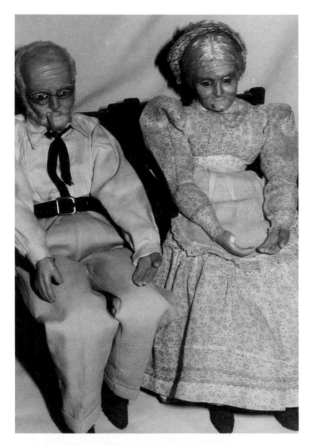

The majority of these wax OLD COUPLE dolls were made in Mexico during the late 1940s and into the 1960s in the town of Pueblo. They were sold through Kimport Dolls as well as other outlets in United States. They were made for export. Both originally held newspapers. The lady can also be holding sewing or knitting. When left out on display, the wax often "aged," making the dolls look older than they actually were. They also came in separate wicker chairs, rockers, or loveseat and chair. Pair - $200.00.

Courtesy Frasher Doll Auction.

8" LIL MISS JENNY is an all vinyl toddler with sleep eyes and rooted hair. Made in Spain by Barval in 1988. $45.00. *Courtesy Kathy Tvrdik.*

Very pretty 15" girl made in Poland in the 1970s. Dressed in original traditional costume. Unmarked. $50.00. *Courtesy Kathy Tvrdik.*

One of the many souvenir dolls that can purchased in Spain. The majority were made in Verdugo-Cadiz by Jose Marlin. Excellent quality and detailing. **$35.00.** *Courtesy Phyllis Kates.*

16" all rigid vinyl doll with painted features and mohair decorated wig. Unjointed with feet attached to wooden stand. Original and is of excellent quality. Part of doll series made and imported in the late 1970s and early 1980s. They were expensive at the time ($75.00 each). Marked "Sandra-Siglo V1X/Marvin Chiclana Espana." **$125.00.** *Courtesy Marie Ernst.*

8" JEANETTE is an all hard plastic walker dressed in a Marcelle Boissier designed outfit. Fortune Toys distributed this doll, but she was made by another company. $65.00. *Courtesy Maureen Fukushima.*

Fortune Toys' most popular doll was PAM, a 7½–8" all hard plastic walker. She is actually a GINGER as were many dolls marketed by Fortune. PAM had several friends her size including JEANETTE and NINETTE, who wore designer clothes. $65.00. *Courtesy Maureen Fukushima.*

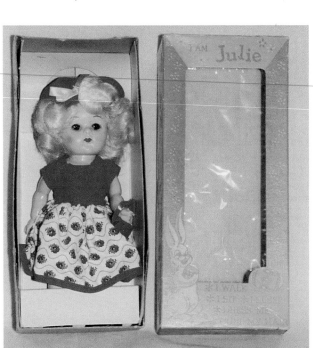

8" all hard plastic JULIE is a walker and a friend of PAM. Both dolls were dressed and marketed by Fortune Toys. $65.00. *Courtesy Maureen Fukushima.*

8" NINETTE in #13/8 "Lounging Ensemble" designed by Michele Cartier. Doll is wide spread leg walker with large round sleep eyes. $65.00. *Courtesy Maureen Fukushima.*

Gerber

The first Gerber Baby was 8" tall and made of all stuffed printed cloth. It came in pink or blue and was on the market until 1939. They are rare and are valued at $400.00.

1954: The Sun Rubber Co. issued a 12" rubber Gerber Baby doll. This doll was an open mouth nurser. The offer for the doll expired in 1955. Few of these have survived in excellent condition due to the rubber drying and collapsing. Sun Rubber made an 18" Gerber Baby for the general market in 1955, as shown in the 1955 Sears catalog. 12" - $225.00; 18" - $300.00.

1966: There was a 14" very soft vinyl baby made by Arrow Industries. It has one deep dimple and a lopsided smile. It actually was not an attractive baby and the offer expired early in 1967. Valued at $65.00.

1972: This was a good year for the Gerber Baby. There was a 10" all firm vinyl baby made by Uneeda Doll Co. The eyes and hair were painted. The baby had either yellow or brown hair. There was also a black version with black molded hair. This was the best received Gerber Baby to that date. Valued at $45.00.

1978: This was the golden anniversary for the Gerber Company and a Gerber Baby was introduced at the New York Toy Fair. Its value is $35.00 up.

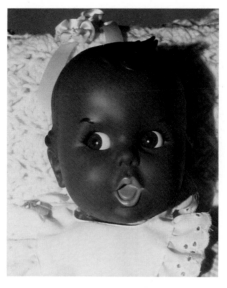

18" reissued GERBER BABY of 1979. Vinyl head and limbs with cloth body. Round, flirty eyes and wide open/closed mouth. Molded hair with front top knot. Black dolls had yellow checkered bodies while white dolls had blue checkered bodies. Made by Atlanta Novelty Co. Black version - $50.00 *Courtesy Jo Merrill.*

Ruth Gibbs

Ruth Gibbs of Farmington, New Jersey, made dolls from the 1940s to 1952. They came in 7", 10", and 12" sizes. The majority of the boxes are marked "Ruth Gibbs Godey's Little Lady Dolls." The doll will be marked "R.G." on back shoulderplate. The doll's designer was Herbert Johnson. Not all Gibbs dolls are Godeys. Many have other names. These dolls have china glazed heads and limbs with pink cloth bodies. They are patterned after the antique china dolls.

10" wigged RUTH GIBBS GODEY'S LITTLE LADY DOLL. Pink luster china with cloth body. China lower limbs with 22K gold painted slippers. Body and limbs are wired to allow posing. Listed in the Ruth Gibbs 1952 brochure. Wigged - $175.00. *Courtesy Susan Giridot.*

12" Ruth Gibbs doll #229 MRS. FITZGERALD IN VISITING DRESS. Shown with two extra gowns and a McCall pattern for the doll. China glazed shoulder head and limbs with cloth body. In box - $200.00. Doll only - $150.00. With wardrobe - $300.00.
Courtesy Christine Green.

Hasbro

12" G.I. JOE MIKE POWER, ATOMIC MAN has scar on cheek and "atomic" arm and leg, plus "atomic flashing eye." Clothes are original. Marked "Hasbro Ind. Inc. 1975/ Made in Hong Kong" on head; "G.I. Joe/ Copyright 1964/Pat #" on back. $175.00 up.
Courtesy Don Tvrdik.

Above: G.I. Joe CRASH CREW FIRE TRUCK, 25x12½x12", included silver firefighter suit. Battery-operated pump sprays water. $125.00 up.

Right: 12" TALKING G.I. JOE issues orders when pull tag in chest is activated. All original. $185.00 up.

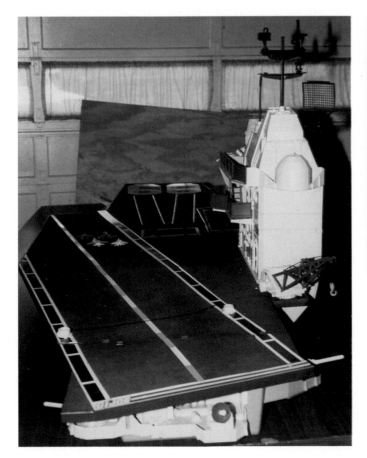

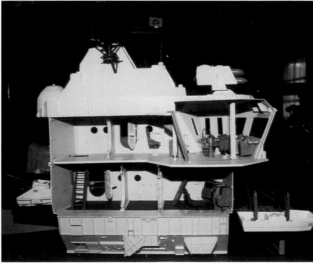

G.I. JOE aircraft carrier, U.S. FLAGG, was on the market in 1982 only. The carrier is 7 feet 6 inches overall, 3 feet wide, and 32 inches tall to top of antenna. Has 64 inch recovery deck and 36-inch catapult launch deck. The carrier has several operating wenches, a flight deck lowering area, a crane, and a launching life boat. Scaled for the smaller G.I. JOE figures. Of all accessories made for G.I. JOE, this carrier is the most difficult item to locate. $650.00 up.

12" NEW KIDS ON THE BLOCK dolls made by Hasbro in 1990–1991. Top row, left to right: DANNY, JOE, and DONNIE. Bottom row: JORDAN and JONATHAN. All have molded earring except JOE. DANNY, JOE, and JORDAN have painted smiles. DONNIE and JONATHAN have serious expressions. All are marked "Big Step Pro., Inc./By Hasbro." Each - $40.00. *Courtesy Kathy Tvrdik.*

Talking URKEL from the TV comedy, *Family Matters*. Vinyl and cloth with painted hair and features. Pull string operated. Made by Hasbro in 1991. $50.00. *Courtesy Jeannie Mauldin.*

5" all vinyl LOVE A BYE BABY with painted features and rooted hair. Fully jointed and original. Marked "Hasbro 1987." $8.00. *Courtesy Kathy Tvrdik.*

8" all vinyl clown with painted face. All original. Marked "Hedaga & Co. Inc. 1967." Pants tagged "Holiday Fair/Made in Japan." $6.00. *Courtesy Kathy Tvrdik.*

12" MISS PIGGY has a felt body and vinyl head with painted features and rooted hair. Original. Created for Henson Assoc. 1989 and made by Direct Connect International, Inc. $25.00. *Courtesy Kathy Tvrdik.*

16" MISS PIGGY hand puppet designed and licensed by Jim Henson from 1976 to 1978. Made of vinyl and satin with inset plastic eyes and rooted hair. $40.00. *Courtesy Kathy Tvrdik.*

⌒ Hollywood Dolls ⌒

The founder of Hollywood Dolls was Domenick Ippolite who put more dolls on the market in 15 years than most doll manufacturers do in a lifetime. They are well marked and came in painted bisque, composition, and hard plastic. Just like the Nancy Ann Storybook Dolls, the Hollywood Dolls are very difficult to identify without original tags and/or box.

All hard plastic LADY GUINEVERE is a Hollywood Doll purchased between 1949 and 1952. She is one of the Princess Series. $30.00 up. *Courtesy Sharon Hamilton.*

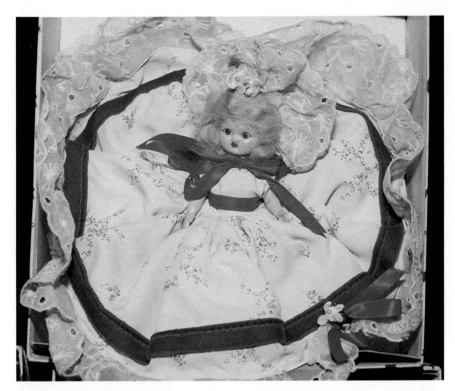

LADY ELAINE made by Hollywood Dolls. Part of the Princess Series. $30.00.
Courtesy Sharon Hamilton.

Hollywood Doll's QUEEN FOR A DAY. $50.00. *Courtesy Sharon Hamilton.*

14" LIL CHARMER from 1968. All vinyl with sleep eyes and rooted hair. Very posable crawling baby. Original. $20.00. *Courtesy Pat Graff.*

20" CHUBBY RUTHIE with composition head and soft vinyl limbs. Glued-on wig and sleep eyes/lashes. Original dress. Missing coat, bonnet, shoes, and socks. Marked "Horsman" on head. From 1950. $65.00. *Courtesy private collection.*

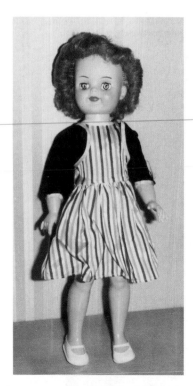

18" CINDY RUTH in 1957, PEGGY ANN, SUB-TEEN in 1959, and GROWN UP MISS in 1960. Plastic and vinyl with rooted hair and sleep eyes. Original except shoes. Marked "Horsman" on head. $95.00. *Courtesy Helena Street.*

11" doll tagged I'M COOKIE, THE CLUB COVER GIRL. Also sold as RUTHIE in 1966. Vinyl and plastic with rooted hair and sleep eyes. All original and in excellent condition. $45.00. *Courtesy Pat Graff.*

30" SIMON SEZ of 1973 has the same head used by WILLI SAYS of 1978. Can be confusing. Plastic head and body with vinyl hands. Cloth arms and legs with sewn on black high top shoes. Molded hair, painted eyes, and puppet mouth that is operated by string in back of head. Original. Marked "Horsman Dolls Inc. 1973" on head. $50.00. *Courtesy Genie Jinright.*

PIPPI LONGSTOCKING dolls. All have freckles. Top: All cloth doll from the movie. Yarn hair and painted features. Made by Applause in 1988. $35.00. Center: 11" plastic and vinyl doll with painted eyes and teeth. Marked "Horsman 1972." $30.00. Bottom: 18" plastic and vinyl doll with painted eyes and teeth. Marked "Horsman 1972." $40.00. *Courtesy Jeannie Mauldin.*

Left: 17" VIOLET PICKLES. Right: 17" RUBY BUTTONS. Both are characters from the *Ivy Cottage* books by E.J. Taylor. Vinyl heads, cloth body and limbs. Made in 1988 by Horsman. Each - $25.00. *Courtesy Pat Graff.*

14" MARY HOYER doll made of all composition with brown eyes. Juliet style dress made from Mary Hoyer pattern. $475.00 up. *Courtesy Jeannie Nespoli.*

14" all composition MARY HOYER with mohair wig and eyes painted to side. In original box with original clothes. (Some dolls were sold with just panties, socks, and shoes. Owner could dress doll in crocheted outfits from MARY HOYER patterns.) $500.00.

Courtesy Susan Giradot.

Beautiful 14" all hard plastic MARY HOYER wearing original tagged riding outfit. Has dynel wig, sleep eyes, and dark sprayed eyeshadow. In mint condition. $525.00. *Courtesy Susan Giradot.*

14" hard plastic MARY HOYER wearing original factory tagged dress. $425.00 up.

14" all hard plastic SOUTHERN BELLE MARY HOYER came with instructions and material for dress and umbrella. This was one of the kit outfits and dolls sold by the company. $425.00 up. *Courtesy Kris Lundquist.*

⌐ Howdy Doody ⌐

The Howdy Doody Show ran on NBC from December 1947 to September 1960 with over 2,500 shows. This show was not designed to teach but for fun. Millions of children, who are now between 50 and 60 years old, were brought up watching Howdy Doody.

The creator of the show was Robert E. Smith, who was the voice of Howdy Doody. Since many of the followers of this series are toy and doll collectors now, they might enjoy the story of Howdy Doody once again.

Twins were born on December 27, 1947, in Texas. They were named Howdy and Double Doody. They lived on a ranch for six years when their rich uncle Doody died and left them some New York City property. Double wanted to stay on the ranch, but Howdy saw his chance to fulfill his dreams. When NBC wanted to purchase his New York property to build a television studio, Howdy agreed but only if they would build him a circus. Bob

Smith, called Buffalo, was appointed Howdy's guardian. (Smith got his nickname from his birthplace, Buffalo, New York.)

The show centered around a circus troupe trying to perform against all the bad things villian Phineas T. Bluster could dream up. Phineas was a mean old man in his 70s who dedicated his life to keeping anyone from having fun. Characters and the actors playing the parts on the shows included the Story Princess, played by Arlene Anderson, Princess Summer-Fall-Winter-Spring, played by Judy Tyler, and Clarabell Hornblower, the popular mute clown. The other characters were puppets like Howdy. They included his cousin Heidi, who was a main circus attraction, Dilly Dally, who could wiggle his ears, and Flubadub.

All in all, this red-headed, freckled puppet gave hours of enjoyment to a generation of American children.

25" HOWDY DOODY ventriloquist doll with mouth operated by a pull string out the back of neck. The head is hard plastic with sleep eyes. The body is cloth. Legs, upper arms, and hands are vinyl. His name is printed on his scarf. Made by Ideal Toy Corp. He also came in 18" and 20" versions. Shown with two 17" HOWDY DOODY marionettes. Strings operate the limbs and mouth. Doll on right has painted eyes and a gap between front teeth. One in foreground has rotating disc eyes. Both are unmarked but may have been made by Ideal. All were made between 1949 and 1958. 25" - $175.00; 17" - $145.00 each. *Courtesy Turn of Century Antiques.*

9" CLARABELL THE CLOWN from the *Howdy Doody Show.* Has terry cloth body with bean bag legs. Vinyl head attached to cloth top with name imprinted on front. Unmarked. $12.00. *Courtesy Kathy Tvrdik.*

⮞Ideal Doll Company⮜

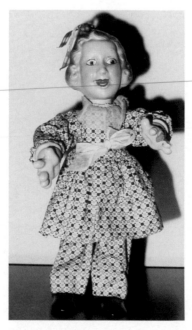

13" BABY SNOOKS from 1938. Has composition head with molded hair and painted eyes. Flexy body has wire tubing for limbs. Fannie Brice character designed by Joseph Kallus. Has original clothes. Original price tag of $1.19. $285.00. *Courtesy Susan Giradot.*

This 17½" mystery doll is all original except for replaced straw hat that is an exact replica. The flowers are stapled to hair. Has a TONI face with sleep eyes. Marked "P-19." Price unknown. *Courtesy private collection.*

21" Miss U.S.O. using the Judy Garland/Deanna Durbin doll from the mid 1940s. Made of all composition with blonde wig and brown sleep eyes. During World War II, this doll was used for Miss America in four sizes, Red Cross Nurse in 12", 14", 18", and 21" sizes, military dolls, and other dolls that were part of the Patriotic Series. Marked with a backward "21" on back. In this condition - $1,000.00 up. *Courtesy Patricia Wood.*

Rare 25" Deanna Durbin in mint condition. All original with black lace gloves and frame hat. Has brown human hair wig and brown sleep eyes. This particular doll may be one of the Miss America or Miss Liberty dolls of the 1940s. $1,200.00 up. *Courtesy Patricia Wood.*

Very beautiful 14" MISS CURITY using the TONI doll with heavy eye makeup and saran wig. All original and in mint condition. Shown with two 7½–8" MISS CURITY dolls with one-piece body and legs. They have sleep eyes with painted lashes and painted-on white socks/shoes. This same doll was used as MARY HARTLINE with red boot trim on calves. All made by Ideal. 14" - $350.00 up; 8" - $90.00 each. *Courtesy Peggy Millhouse.*

14" brunette TONI in tagged dress with Toni play wave set. Made of hard plastic with sleep eyes. TONI dolls came in all hair colors. Marked "P-90." Mint in box - $400.00 up. *Courtesy Susan Giradot.*

14" TONI WALKER with platinum wig, original dress, and Ideal marked plastic shoes. Marked "P-90." $325.00 up. *Courtesy Susan Giradot.*

19" TONI made of hard plastic with nylon wig and sleep eyes. Clothes may be original. They are of the right era. Marked "P-92." $475.00 up. *Courtesy Sharon McDowell.*

19" TONI made of hard plastic with nylon wig. All original. Marked "P-92." $475.00 up. *Courtesy Sharon McDowell.*

15" "P-91" and 18" "P-93" TONI dolls made of hard plastic with sleep eyes. Both are all original and in mint condition. P-91 - $375.00; P-93 - $500.00. *Courtesy Kris Lundquist.*

23" P-94 is the rarest doll in the TONI series. P-94 TONI dolls have nylon wigs. If she has a saran or dynel wig or has heavily curled or hard to comb hair, she is a MARY HARTLINE doll, as pictured. MARY HARTLINE usually has her name and music imprinted on her dress. Mary Hartline's character appeared in ABC's "Super Circus" TV show in the early 1950s. Toni - $650.00; Mary Hartline - $750.00. *Courtesy June Schultz.*

This 21" P-93 TONI is hard to find. Clothes are tagged and doll is marked. All original and in mint condition. A wonderful example of this size TONI. $600.00.

Courtesy Jeannie Nespoli.

Rare 16" MARY HARTLINE with vinyl head, sleep eyes, and rooted, side-parted saran wig. Has hard plastic TONI body. Original MARY HARTLINE dress in white. It also came in red, green, and blue. Mint condition - $475.00. *Courtesy Susan Giradot.*

10" all vinyl LITTLE MISS REVLON with jointed waist, sleep eyes, and rooted hair. All original. Marked "Ideal Doll/VT-10." From 1957. $90.00 up. *Courtesy Ann Wencel.*

10" original LITTLE MISS REVLON in mint condition. Tag states "The youngest member of the famous Revlon Family." Marked "Ideal Doll/VT-10." From 1957. $90.00 up. *Courtesy Ann Wencel.*

10" all vinyl LITTLE MISS REVLON with jointed waist and high heel feet. All original and in mint condition. Marked "Ideal Doll/VT-10." $90.00 up. *Courtesy Maureen Fukushima.*

22" all hard plastic SAUCY WALKER with pin-jointed hips. When she walks, her head turns from side to side when hand is held. Has flirty eyes and saran wig. All original with original box. Made from 1951 to 1955. In box - $200.00. *Courtesy Jeannie Mauldin.*

14" SAUCY WALKER is really cute in this tiny size. Just like larger sizes except eyes do not flirt (move from side to side). All original and in mint condition. $85.00. *Courtesy Gloria Anderson.*

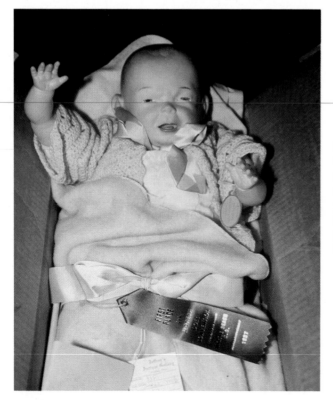

BLESSED EVENT was also advertised as KISS ME. Has vinyl head and lower limbs with oil cloth body and upper limbs. Newborn face with molded tongue and painted eyes. Facial expressions change when plunger in back is pressed. All original with arm tag. In original box mailed from Sears with sales slip of $9.98 Came in 19" and 21" sizes in 1950. $165.00. *Courtesy Jeannie Mauldin.*

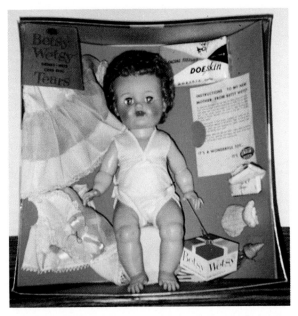

17" PRINCESS MARY with head made of early vinyl that usually turned darker than later made vinyl. Has sleep eyes and hair lashes. Hair pulled back into bun. All original except for shoes. Came in 16", 17", 19", and 21" sizes and was on TONI body. Both plain and walker bodies were used. Can be marked along with "Ideal Doll/VT-17, W-18 or V-87." $95.00 up.

This 13" BETSY WETSY was made in late 1956 and into 1957. Has tightly curled saran rooted hair in vinyl head. Vinyl body and limbs. Nurser with open mouth. Came packaged as shown with layette attached to inside box lid. This particular dress also came in yellow and pastel green. Marked "Ideal Doll/VW-2." $75.00. *Courtesy Mike Way.*

14" BETSY WETSY with hard plastic head and all vinyl body. Nurser with open mouth. After drinking, the stomach can be pressed and doll will cry tears and nose will run. All original in box with layette. This model was made from 1954 through 1956. Came in this box as well as a window box. First ones will be marked with patent number. Others marked "Made in USA" along with "Ideal Doll." Doll only - $25.00; mint in box - $90.00.

Courtesy Ellyn McCorkell.

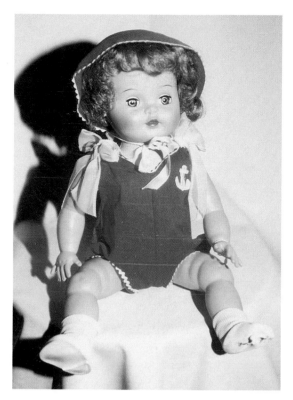

20" PATTI PRAYS has vinyl face and hands, cloth body, plush white hair, and painted features. Identified by ribbon tag pinned to printed pajamas. She recites "Now I Lay Me Down To Sleep" by turning crank in her back. Doll can kneel and clasp her hands in prayer. Made in 1957 only and sold for $3.99. $50.00.

Courtesy Susan Giradot.

18" CREAM PUFF of 1959 is made of all vinyl with closed mouth and sleep eyes. All original. Marked "Ideal/OB-19-2" on head and "Ideal Toy Corp./19. 1961." on back. The other CREAM PUFF versions (1960–1962) had a "watermelon slice" style mouth with same body. This particular doll was also used as BABY COOS in 1959. $50.00.

Is it any wonder the PATTI PLAYPAL dolls are so desirable to collectors? These beautiful 35" dolls are plastic with vinyl heads and hands. They are jointed at the wrists and have sleep eyes. Heads and legs are strung. Rooted saran hair can be straight or curly. Blondes are found most often but they also came with brunette and orange-red hair. Black hair is rare. Made in 1959 to 1961. **$285.00 each.** *Courtesy Shirley Merrill.*

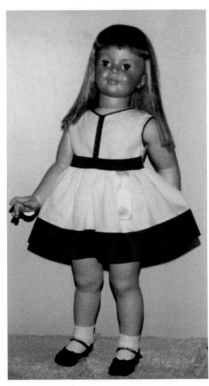

35" PATTI PLAYPAL with long straight hair and sleep eyes. Head and legs are strung. Wearing original dress with attached half slip. Rayon label on skirt reads "Patti Playpal." Marked "G 35-7." $285.00 up.

Courtesy Ann Wencel.

28" SUSIE PLAYPAL made of all vinyl with rooted saran hair and sleep eyes. Has oversized hands. There was also a blonde version. Marked "Ideal Doll/OEB-28-5" and "Ideal" in oval on back. Made in 1960. All original and in mint condition. $125.00. *Courtesy Jeannie Mauldin.*

Elusive 38" PETER PLAYPAL was made in 1960 and 1961. Has side part hairdo that came in several shades. Brunettes are difficult to find. He walks while holding his hand. Marked "BE-35-38" along with "Ideal Toy Corp." on the head and "Ideal Toy Corp./W-38/Pat. Pend." on body. $425.00. *Courtesy Shirley Merrill.*

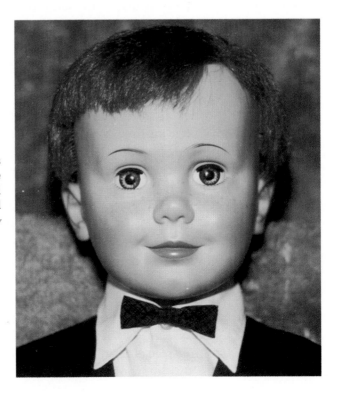

32" and 28" SAUCY WALKER from 1960 and 1961. They were a part of the PATTI PLAYPAL family and came in various outfits. Both have rooted saran hair and sleep eyes. Marked "Ideal Toy Corp/Bye 32-35" on head and "Ideal Toy Corp./B-32-W Pat. Pend" on body. Each - $150.00 up. *Courtesy Shirley Merrill.*

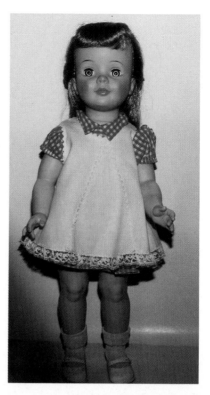

18" all vinyl PATTITE is the smallest member of the PATTI PLAYPAL family. She was made in 1960 and is called LITTLE (PETITE) PATTI by collectors. A walker version was made in 1961. Marked "Ideal Corp./G-18" on head. $95.00 up. *Courtesy Susan Giradot.*

The mystery of Betsy McCall, Miss Ideal, and Terry Twist still continues. The same doll apparently is used for all. Were some Betsy McCall dolls packaged in American Character boxes actually made by Ideal? Apparently so. These Betsy McCall dolls are marked only with "McCall/1961" and are shown in catalogs for Sears and other department stores that same year. They have jointed wrists but does Miss Ideal? The description in Ideal's catalog says they do, but examples do not. This author believes that if the doll has jointed wrists, it is Betsy McCall or Miss Ideal, and only the Terry Twist has unjointed wrists. Since they all came in 25", 29", and 30" sizes, you can take your pick! The markings can be the same: "Ideal Toys Corp./SP-25-S" for 25" dolls or "SP-30-S" for 30" dolls. All these dolls have extra joints at waist and ankles. It is known that since American Character had the Betsy McCall license in 1960, they purchased blanks from Ideal to meet their production demand.

25" TERRY TWIST has unjointed wrists but has extra joints at ankles and waist. Her outfit came in various colors. Marked "Ideal Toy Corp. SP-25-S. 1961." Shown in *Modern Collector Dolls, Sixth Series,* as MISS IDEAL who has the same markings. $375.00. *Courtesy Cris Johnson.*

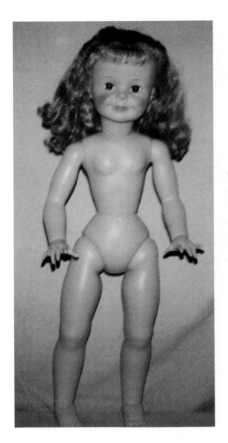

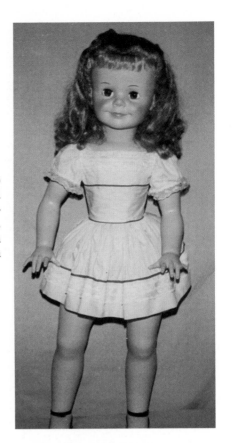

This 30" doll has unjointed wrists so most likely she is TERRY TWIST, but could certainly be MISS IDEAL. Does have jointed waist and ankles. All original. Marked "Ideal Toy Corp./SP-30-S" on head and "Ideal Toy Corp./G-32-S" on back. **$375.00.** *Courtesy private collection.*

Carol Brent was to Montgomery Wards as Betty Crocker was to General Mills – a made up advertising personality and symbol. Ideal produced a 15" doll in 1961, and she was marked "Ideal Toy Corp./ML" on her head and "Ideal Toy Corp/M-15" on the body.

There was also a 15" Jackie using the same doll and some of the Carol Brent clothing. She is marked "VT-10" or "VT-10½" on her head, and the body is marked the same as the Carol Brent doll.

To add confusion to the topic, in 1962 another doll with the same markings as Carol Brent was made. Her name was Liz or Fashion Liz. She was sold in a swimsuit and had heavy eye make-up. She had eight special outfits made for her in high fashion (haute couture) style. Her hair is styled either on top of her head or shoulder length. She has very beautiful hands. This doll is hard to find in original condition.

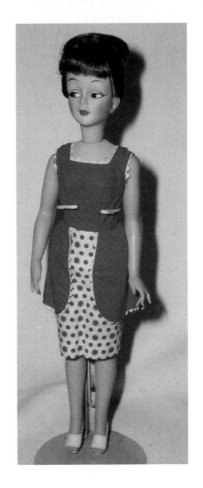

15" CAROL BRENT has eyes painted to side and hair styled on top of head. Marked "Ideal Toy Corp./ML" on head; "Ideal Toy Corp./M-15" on body. Made in 1961. In mint condition - $75.00 up.

15" CAROL BRENT from 1961. Plastic body, vinyl head and limbs. Eyes painted to side. Has high heel feet. Original. Marked "Ideal Toy Corp./M-15-L" on head and "Ideal Toy Corp./M-15" on body. $75.00 up.

15" JACKIE also came in 19" and 21" sizes. Has sleep eyes, rooted saran hair, and high heel feet. Hair styled up as well as shoulder length. Marked "Ideal You Corp G-15-L" on head. Some may be marked "M-15-1" along with Ideal name. Shown in 1961 Ideal catalog. $75.00 up. *Courtesy David Spurgeon.*

~ Tammy ~

Tammy was released in 1962 as "the doll you love to dress." During this time, many American mothers thought Barbie was "too much" doll for their child to play with, and Ideal felt perhaps Tammy would be the answer to the teen doll dilemma. She was designed not to be as old nor as buxom as Barbie. Tammy's clothes told her story as a typical middle class high school girl and your favorite girl next door or babysitter. The names of her outfits, such as "Sorority Sweetheart," "Picnic Party," and "School Daze," projected this image. While Barbie was the high fashion model in high heel shoes, Tammy wore flats and low heel pumps. (Mattel did let Barbie settle down, go to college, and do less modeling in 1964.) As Tammy grew up, her head became thinner and her clothes become more sophisticated, yet she was still a "little girl" compared to Barbie.

The American family was the main concept behind Tammy and her family. Because of the nation's obsession with the perfect TV family in the 1960s, Ideal developed the "ideal" homelife for Tammy. Much like "Ozzie & Harriet," "The Donna Reed Show," and "Father Knows Best," Tammy had a family unit consisting of a 13" father, a 12½" mother, 12½" brother Ted, 8" sister Pepper, and 9" Dodi, Pepper's friend. As Tammy and her family increased in popularity, Mattel tamed Barbie even more.

By 1965, there was a changing mood in American girls. With the Beatles hitting American shores, Tammy left the doll scene, leaving Barbie to become more "*mod*-ern."

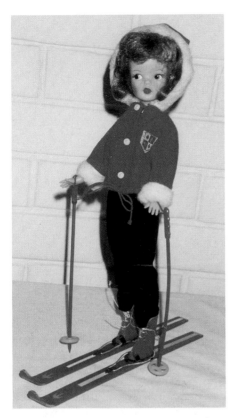

12" TAMMY with painted features. Dressed in all original #9211 "Snow Bunny" outfit from 1962. $50.00.

Courtesy Pat Graff.

8" all vinyl PEPPER, little sister to TAMMY. Painted features and freckles. Original first issue. Extra outfits were available. Marked "P9-3" on head. From 1963–1964. $40.00. *Courtesy Karen Geary.*

13½" TAMMY'S FATHER and 12½" GROWN UP TAMMY. Both are original, but father is missing his shoes. He is marked "Ideal Toy Corp./M-13-2" on head and "Ideal Toy Corp/B-12½/2" on body. He has graying temples and bears strong resemblance to Robert Young of "Father Knows Best." $60.00 each. *Courtesy Kathy Tvrdik.*

8" PEPPER marked "Ideal Doll Corp./P9-3" on head, but it can also be "G9-3." Along with the Ideal name, the doll can be marked on back "G9-W" or "DO-P." Pepper and her friend, DODI, used the same body. Has freckles. Shown with 12" TAMMY wearing one of her favorite outfits. From 1962. 8" - $40.00; 12" - $50.00.

Courtesy Kathy Tvrdik.

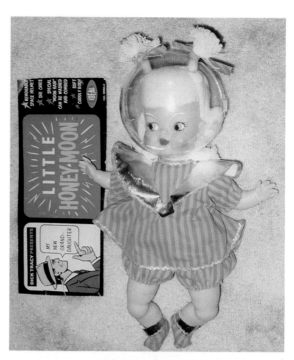

9" all vinyl Tearie Dearie is an open nurser. First dolls used Betsy Wetsy body of 1957 with index finger on right hand held high and third finger curled in. This outfit came with baby bottle if from 1965. Doll made from 1963 through 1967. Marked "Ideal Toy Co./BW-9-4." $30.00. *Courtesy Susan Giridot.*

Little Honeymoon wearing her original plastic space helmet. She is unplayed with condition. End of box shows Dick Tracy proudly stating, "My new Granddaughter." Marked "1965 C.T.-N.YN. S./Ideal Toy Corp./HM/4-2-2H." With helmet - $65.00. *Courtesy Chris McWilliams.*

23" Bibsy made of all heavy vinyl with rooted hair and small holes in ears. When squeezed, mouth closes and she makes squeaky noise. Marked "Ideal Toy Corp/D-20-1" on head and "Ideal Toy Corp/D/23" on back. From 1969. In mint condition - $55.00. *Courtesy Phyllis Houston-Kates.*

16" Tiny Kissy is very unusual with her side-parted long hair. Same plastic and vinyl body as other Kissy dolls. Wearing original dress. Marked "Ideal Toy Corp./K-16-1" on head and "Ideal Toy Corp./K-16/3" on back. Made 1961–1967. $40.00. *Courtesy Marie Ernst.*

8" TEEN FLATSY dolls are made of ¼" cut vinyl. Posable with rooted hair and painted features. Green haired doll is GWEN THE STUDENT. In box with blue hair is DALE THE ACTRESS. The other two in the series are ALI THE CITY GIRL with orange hair and CORY THE MODEL with pink hair. Made 1970–1972. Each - $15.00. *Courtesy private collection.*

4½" FLATSY dolls were introduced in 1969 with a series of nine figures. By 1971, 12 more dolls were added to the collection plus the 8½" teen and 2½" mini dolls. Shown is one of the last FLATSY dolls called SPINDERELLA. She is mounted on base and when string is pulled, she spins around. $22.00. *Courtesy Kathy Tvrdik.*

15½" black LOOK AROUND VELVET made by Ideal in 1972. All original in tagged Velvet outfit. In mint condition - $50.00 up. *Courtesy Pat Graff.*

TWIRLY CURLS CRISSY from 1974. Has one long hair braid down back. Dressed in special Christmas outfit and offered to a large chain store as a special. When declined by store, all 624 dolls made were sold through Coast To Coast stores. In this outfit - $60.00.

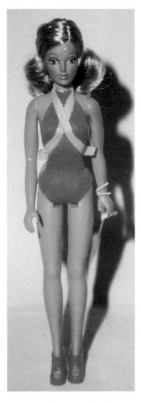

11½" TUESDAY TAYLOR BEAUTY QUEEN as she was when first offered for sale in 1978. She is one of the prettiest 11½" adult figures to be on market for some years. Made of vinyl and plastic with sunstreaked hair. All original and in mint condition. She also came as a Super Model. Marked "1977 Ideal" in oval and "H-293 Hong Kong." $40.00.

12" JEANETTE CHIPETTE, friend of Alvin and The Chipmunks. Cloth body with vinyl head and lower limbs. Painted features and purple plastic glasses. (There were two other chipmunk girls in the series. ELEANOR was chubby with eyes painted to side and BRITTANY had eyes painted upward and to the side.) Head marked "1984 Karman Ross. Prod. Inc./Mfd by CBS, Inc." with "Ideal" in oval, and "11-437." Body tagged "1984 CBS Toys Div. CBS Inc. Newark, N.J." Original - $30.00. *Courtesy Kathy Tvrdik.*

International Tribal Dolls

International Tribal Doll Inc. of Los Angeles, California, had the exclusive manufacturing and distributing rights for a Fulani Tribe doll and applied for its U.S. patent in 1986.

The 18" doll has hair braided with beads, sea shells, and gold strings. She also has sleep eyes and vinyl facial decorations. Made in China, the doll came with a video tape and a 14-page booklet describing the Fulani Tribe of West Africa. There was suppose to be a series of these dolls, but they never reached the market. The dolls made were eventually sold through overstock distributors.

18" Fulani made by International Tribal Doll, Inc. Came with video and 14-page booklet. $125.00. *Courtesy David Spurgeon.*

⮎ Irwin ⮌

Irwin Plastics made blank dolls for anyone that wanted them. They even made dolls and talcum containers in the image of dolls for Ideal Doll Company, Mollye International, Knickerbocker, Famous Thread Co. (a crochet and patterns company), Elaina Baby Accessory Company, and many others. Irwin dolls can be distinguish by their wide open hands. If dolls cannot be identified by the exact company marketing them, it is correct to say they are Irwin dolls. Their value will the be the same no matter who distributed them.

6½" pull string walker made for Bal Dolls, Inc. by Irwin Plastics. All hard plastic with open hands. The palm is shown forward on one hand; back of the hand is shown forward on the other. Has large feet with molded-on shoes. Original felt helmet and majorette costume. (Flocked design on costume is badly worn.) Clothes are stapled on. This particular model came in 10–11" sizes. Bal Dolls, Inc. also made molded hairdos, some under the wigs. Doll walks when molded loop on stomach is pulled. $15.00.

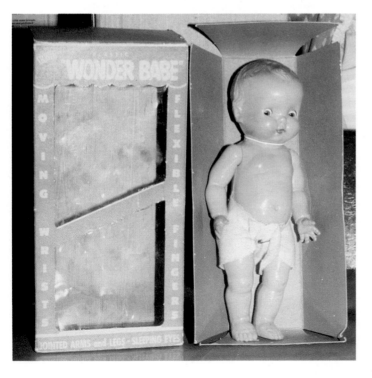

6" WONDER BABE by Irwin Plastics with one-piece body and head. Sleep eyes on rockers that "sleep" very loosely. Original in box. Can be dressed by owner or played with, as is, by child. $15.00. *Courtesy David Spurgeon.*

~ Kenner ~

12" C-3P0 and 7½" R2-D2 from the *Star Wars* movie series. Both are all plastic and jointed. Made in 1974. In mint condition. Each - $150.00. *Courtesy Don Tvrdik.*

5" STRAWBERRY SHORTCAKE with cat CUSTARD and strawberry-shaped sleeping bag. Vinyl head with rooted hair and sleep eyes. Shown in original box. Marked "American Greeting/Made in Hong Kong." Made in 1984 only. $25.00.

∼ Strawberry Shortcake ∼

The first Strawberry Shortcake dolls were made in 1980 and were based on characters appearing on American Greeting Cards. Each doll came with a pet that carried a scent to match the dolls' names. There were 12 dolls in the the series, and each were 4½–5" tall, except for the baby that was 3½" tall. Markings on items will be "American Greeting Corp. Kenner Products" or "CPG Products Corp." and dated 1980 to 1984. They are presently valued at $12.00 each. The following is a list of the original dolls and their pets:

Strawberry Shortcake and Custard	Blueberry Muffin and Cheesecake
Huckleberry Pie (boy) and Pupcake	Lime Chiffon and Parfait Parrot
Raspberry Tart and Rhubarb	Cherry Cobbler and Gooseberry
Orange Blossom (black) and Marmalade	Apple Dumplin' and Tea Time Turtle
Lemon Meringue and Frappé	Angel Cake and Soufflé
Apricot (baby) and Hopsalot	Butter Cookie and Jelly Bear

Listed in 1980 is a character called T.N. Honey with blonde hair that wears glasses, a green and white striped dress, and a hat with a "smiley face" sunflower tie pin. It is not know if she was ever produced.

Each of the dolls had extra outfits that could be purchased. There were eight outfits for the large dolls and four for the babies. There were also "friendly foes" introduced on the market in 1982. They were 8½" Pieman and Berry Bird and Sourgrapes and Dregs, a snake. These figures are valued at $15.00 each.

In 1982, ten new Party Pleaser dolls were put on the shelves. These dolls were 3¾–5" tall and each had a pet. They also carried the scent of their name. Their current value is $4.00 each. Listed are the Party Pleaser Strawberry Shortcake dolls and pets:

Strawberry Shortcake and Custard	Cafe Olé with Burrito
Orange Blossom with Marmalade	Almond Tea and Marza Panda
Mint Tulip and Marsh Mallard	Plum Puddin' and Elderberry Owl
Peach Blush and Melonie Belle	Cherry Cobbler and Gooseberry
Angel Cake and Soufflé	Apple Dumplin' and Tea Time Turtle

In 1983, Kenner added Fig Boot, a little purple beasty, and the twins Lem and Ada with Sugarwoofer. Also released was Strawberry Ballerina that came with a special outfit and accessories. In 1984, five Sweet Sleepers were added to the Strawberry Shortcake line. Each had sleep eyes and came packaged with sleeping bag and pet. They are valued at $25.00 each. They included Shortberry Shortcake and Custard, Raspberry Tart and Rhubarb, Orange Blossom and Marmalade, Blueberry Muffin and Cheesecake, and Lemon Meringue and Frappé.

Between 1980 and 1984, there were enough Strawberry Shortcake and friends produced to keep collectors busy for a long, long time. Riding on the popularity of the first dolls, Kenner flooded the market with a vast amout of merchandise and licensed much more to be made. To meet consumer demands, they over-manufactured and the market reached its saturation point fast. Instead of pacing the demand, Kenner released so much merchandise that buyers could not keep up with it all and stopped buying. To illustrate the overproduction, this is what Kenner released in three years: six 13–15" cloth dolls in first set (second set added three more), six 15" cloth and vinyl babies in two sets, four drink-and-wet dolls, 10 plush animals, 36 scented miniature figures, many vehicles, several carry cases, playsets, doll houses, and storybooks, a buggy, and a bassinet. For the person who liked everything, there was bedding, drapes, furniture, clocks, dishes, lamps, Halloween costumes, painting books, and games to complement the dolls. Much like Mattel's Kiddles, it is hard to find Strawberry Shortcakes in complete sets.

Left: LEWIS TULLY from early set of the GHOSTBUSTERS. Right: PETER VENKMAN with eyes that bug out, jaw that drops, and hair that raises. Marked "Columbia Pictures." Made from 1987 to 1989. Each - $18.00. *Courtesy Don Tvrdik.*

Left: RAY STANTZ of the GHOSTBUSTERS. His eyes and hair raise and ears extend. Right: WINSTON ZEDDMORE has a mouth that opens and head that rotates 360 degrees. Made by Kenner from 1987 to 1989. Each - $18.00. *Courtesy Don Tvrdik.*

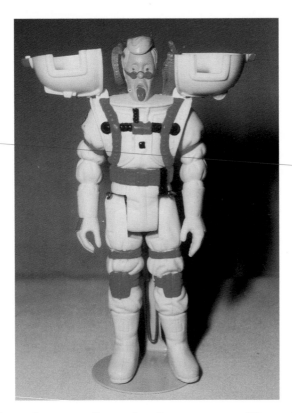

EGON SPENGLER from the GHOSTBUSTERS. His neck extends, jaw drops, and tie pops up in the 1988 version. On this 1987 version, his helmet pops open and hair flips up. Kenner made Ghostbuster figures, buildings, and vehicles from 1987 to 1989. $20.00.

Courtesy Don Tvrdik.

Left: GRANNY GROSS with mouth that flies open, her hat goes into air, and eyes spin. Right: JANINE with eyes that bug out, jaw that drops open, and her fore-lock flips out. Both are from the movie *Ghostbusters* and marked "Columbia Pictures." Made in 1987 to 1989. Each - $25.00. *Courtesy Don Tvrdik.*

5" FLASH GORDON and MING, his arch enemy. Both have cupped hands to hold weapons and levers on back to operate arms. Clothes molded on. MING has cloth cape. Each - $15.00. *Courtesy Don Tvrdik.*

5" PHANTOM and MANDRAKE, THE MAGICIAN as Defenders of Earth from the FLASH GORDON set. Weapons fit into either hand on figures. Molded-on clothes and hat. Marked "KFE/KFS." From 1986. Each - $15.00. *Courtesy Don Tvrdik.*

8" HACKER, Dr. Terror's henchman from Centurions Power Xtreme series. He is half man, half cyborg. From 1986. $25.00. *Courtesy Don Tvrdik.*

13" plastic and vinyl COOL CUT KARA with open/closed mouth and painted eyes. Shown in original box. Came with scissors, extra hair pieces, comb, stand, and instructions for different hairstyles. Marked "Kenner 1990." $40.00. *Courtesy Kathy Tvrdik.*

Left to right: 17" TALKING URKEL by Hasbro in 1991; 18½" TALKING PEE-WEE HERMAN by Matchbox in 1987; 19" ED GRIMLY by Tyco in 1989; 16" BEETLEJUICE by Kenner in 1989; 19" TALKING FREDDY KRUGER by Matchbox in 1989; 16½" TALKING ERNEST by Kenner in 1989. Each - $50.00. *Courtesy David Spurgeon.*

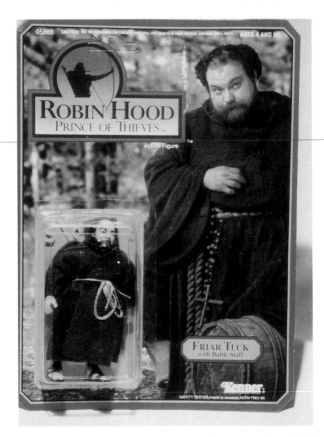

5" FRIAR TUCK from the movie *Robin Hood*. Made by Kenner in 1992. Most difficult character to find from set. $20.00.

11½" TALENT SHOW RAQUEL from MISS AMERICA doll collection made by Kenner in 1991. Baton twisting "Yankee Doodle Twirler." Plastic and vinyl with painted features and bendable legs. All original. Other dolls in series are TANYA, BLAIR, DEVON, and JUSTINE. $40.00. *Courtesy Kathy Tvrdik.*

22" BLAIR (left) and LAUREN (right) from the ALWAYS SISTERS series made by Kenner in 1988. Both are vinyl with cloth bodies and have extra joints at knees, ankles, and elbows for posing. BLAIR has purple inset eyes/lashes; LAUREN has blue inset eyes/lashes. Blair's outfit has a matching tam (not shown.) Both are original and in mint condition. Each - $35.00. *Courtesy Pat Graff.*

Three 17" dolls from JETSETTERS collection made by Lanard Toys in 1988. They are KENYA (left), NIKITA (center), and LEILANI (right). Each are vinyl with painted eyes and jointed waists. (See other two JETSETTERS dolls in *Modern Collector's Dolls, Sixth Series.*) All original and in mint condition. Each - $80.00. *Courtesy Pat Graff.*

Lenci

The name Lenci came from the registered trademark's initials: <u>L</u>udus <u>E</u>st <u>N</u>obis <u>C</u>onstanter <u>I</u>ndustria. It is loosely translated as *To play is our constant work.*

Lenci dolls were reintroduced in 1978, and all dolls made have been limited world-wide to 999 editions. The majority of the dolls during the first years of production fell short of this mark. They will be numbered on back of heads, and most clothes will be tagged.

From 1978 to 1983, the space between the first and second fingers was spread quite far apart on all dolls, except for three models. The second and third fingers are sewn together. After 1983, all fingers are sewn together unless the hand is holding something or the entire hand is sewn around an object.

14" PRIMAVERA dressed in organdy with felt flowers. Has large painted "surprise" eyes. Silver Lenci tag sewn to back. Marked "CP123" on head. From 1984. $425.00. *Courtesy Glorya Woods.*

24" MODESTINA with painted "surprise" eyes. Clothes are mostly felt with some organdy. Shown inside original box. From 1984. $550.00. *Courtesy Kathy Tvrdik.*

Left: 13" AURELIA, the reissue of a 1931 doll, was made exclusively for the Enchanted Doll House in 1983. All felt dress with ruffle at hem and organdy apron. Holds felt goose. Clothes and body tagged. Head marked "AS9." Right: 13" ALDO with leather belt and shoes. Head marked "BH 2343." Body tagged "Lenci." Girl - $465.00; boy - $425.00. *Courtesy Glorya Woods.*

13" SERENA made by Lenci in 1990. Eyes painted to side. Wears organdy dress with felt flowers and hat. Dress tagged "Lenci-Torino/New York, Paris & London." Body tagged "Lenci/Mod Depose/Made in Turin, Italy." Shown with 8" MASCOTTE from 1930s. 13" - $425.00; 8" - $365.00. *Courtesy Glorya Woods.*

13" STELLA dressed in felt and organdy. Has flowers on upper hat. Marked "BR 393" on head. $425.00. *Courtesy Glorya Woods.*

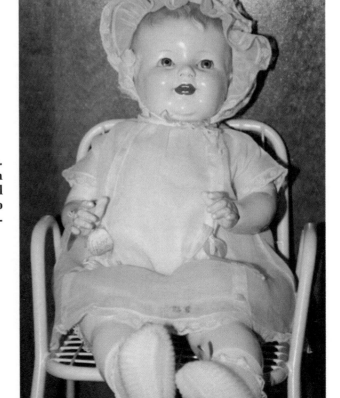

26" HAPPY BABY made by Libby Dolls of New York in 1935. Made of composition and cloth with tin sleep eyes. Open mouth with two upper teeth and two lower teeth. All original with wrist tag. Dolls from this mold were sold to other firms to be dressed and marketed. In mint condition - $265.00. *Courtesy Jeannie Mauldin.*

13" battery-operated BUBBLE YUM doll blows "bubble gum" from wide open mouth. Has painted eyes, rooted hair, and non-removable tennis shoes. Marked "Lifesavers, Inc. 1988." $18.00. *Courtesy Kathy Tvrdik.*

7" LION-O (left), SAFARI JOE (center), and evil foe (left) from the THUNDERCATS series. Lever on back of each figure activates arms. Made in 1985 to 1987. LION-O and evil foe are marked "Telpix/Lic. T. Wolf/L.J.N. Toys." SAFARI JOE is marked "L.J.N. 1985 Lic. T. Wolf LJN Toys." Each - $22.00. *Courtesy Don Tvrdik.*

8" World Wrestling Federation (WWF) Superstars made by LJN in 1984 to 1985. Each are made of very bendable vinyl and have molded-on clothes. Top left: Hulk Hogan (left) and WWF announcer, name unknown (right). Top right: "Rowdy" Roddy Piper (left) and Mr. Wonderful (right). Bottom left: Big John Studd (left) and Randy "Macho Man" Savage (right). Bottom right: Brutus Beefcake (left) and Junk Yard Dog (right). Wrestlers - $8.00 each; announcer - $10.00. *Courtesy Don Tvrdik.*

8" IRON SHEIK (left) and unknown black wrestler (right). Both made of bendable vinyl and are marked "LJN Titan Sports." From 1984–1985. Each - $8.00. *Courtesy Don Tvrdik.*

8" CLASSY FREDDIE BLASSIE, WRESTLING SUPERSTARS MANAGER. One-piece construction made of bendable vinyl. Marked "Titan Sports (a trademark of Marvel Comics)/1984 L.J.N., Ltd." $10.00. *Courtesy Don Tvrdik.*

There were over 25 figures in this set and it is not known if all were put on the market. WWF Superstars not shown:

HILLBILLY JIM in coveralls, full beard, and tan molded on hat.

ANDRE THE GIANT with black hair, bikini, and boots.

NIKOLAI VOLKOFF with red body suit, boots, and molded-on black "fur" hat.

GREG VALENTINE with long white hair, black bikini and boot.

KING KONG BUNDY has bald head and dressed in navy blue half body suit with straps, knee pads, and boots.

TITO SANTANA with black hair, dark gray turnks, knee pads, and boots.

GEORGE "THE ANIMAL" STEELE with bald head and dressed in black pants with red stripe, red pads and boots.

RICKY "THE DRAGON" DREAMBOAT with black hair and dressed in black bikini over red leggings and black boots.

JESSIE "THE BODY" VENTURA with white hair, pink leggings and bikini, and blue/white boots.

CORPORAL KIRCHNER dressed in green shirt, camafloge pants, black boots, and burnt orange beret.

CAPT. LOU ALBANO with long black mustache hair and beard around mouth. Dressed in white shirt, black pants, and blue vest.

BOBBY THE BRAIN dressed in blue shirt and black pants and has both thumbs up.

JIMMY HART dressed in red shirt, white jacket with black musical notes, and black pants. Wearing dark glasses.

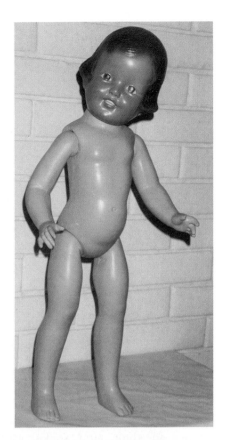

Beautiful 23" character doll made of all composition with big smile and no name. She has excellent teeth detail and hair modeling. Eyes are painted decals. Head looks very much like the "top of the line" from Reliable of Canada. Body is from the SHIRLEY TEMPLE mold from Ideal, which was sold to other companies over the years. The limbs, especially the bent elbow on right arm, seem to be Knickerbocker. (It is not bent enough to be Effanbee.) The clothes appear to be original. Dress length is post World War II style. Unmarked. $250.00 up. *Courtesy Pat Graff.*

11" all composition HENRETTE with three tuffs of hair. In 1930s, many companies made these dolls, and they came in various qualities. Sold as RADIO BABY, SOUTHERN BABY, or the licensed AMOSANDRA from the "Amos and Andy Radio Show." After popularity diminished, an unknown maker produced this doll marked "Henrette/Made in USA/1944." $30.00. *Courtesy Kathy Tvrdik.*

16" SAD SACK was a World War II comic character developed by Sgt. George Baker and appeared in the military magazine, *Stars and Stripes.* He was in 1959 Sears catalog. One-piece body and limbs with molded-on shoes and painted features. Long neck is only joint. Both are original, except one is missing hat. Unmarked. Each - $125.00. *Courtesy Jeannie Mauldin.*

7" CAMPBELL KID made of thin, inexpensive vinyl. Molded-on shoes and socks. Molded hair with painted-on hairbow. Only marks are "1984 Campbell Soup" on head and "26/1984/Campbell Soup" on back. $16.00. *Courtesy Kathy Tvrdik.*

9½" FREDDIE-MAXX FX is a multi-action figure from 1990. Maxx, pictured here as FREDDIE KRUEGER, was also packaged as DRACULA/FRANKENSTEIN and THE ALIEN. Box marked "Matchbox Trademark, The Fourth New Line. 'Nightmare on Elm Street.' Heron Venture. All rights reserved." In package - $20.00; figure only - $8.00. *Courtesy Don Tvrdik.*

11½" CHERYL TIEGS, REAL MODEL was made in 1989 by Matchbox. Plastic and vinyl with bending knees and painted features. Very few of these dolls reached market. $45.00.

11½" CHRISTIE BRINKLEY, REAL MODEL and BEVERLY JOHNSON, REAL MODEL made of plastic and vinyl with bendable knees. Both have painted features. Marked "Matchbox 1989. Made in China." Christie - $45.00; Beverly - $50.00.

❧ Mattel ❧

FRIENDS AND RELATIVES OF BARBIE
1980–1989

1980:
Christie: Beauty Secrets, Kissing, and Sun Lovin'g Malibu. Each - $25.00.
Ken: Sport and Shave - $18.00.
P.J.: Sun Lovin' Malibu - $20.00.
Skipper: Super Teen and Sun Lovin' Malibu. Each - $16.00.
Scott: Skipper's boyfriend. $25.00.

1981:
Christie: Golden Dreams - $35.00.
Ken: Roller Skating - $20.00.

1982:
Christie: Sunsational Malibu - $20.00. Pink & Pretty - $30.00.

Ken: Western - $20.00. All Star - $18.00. Sunsational - $15.00. Malibu (black) - $20.00. Fashion Jeans - $19.00.
P.J.: Sunsational Malibu - $20.00.
Skipper: Sunsational Malibu - $16.00.

1983:
Ken: Dream Date - $28.00. Horse Lovin' - $30.00.
P.J.: Dream Date - $20.00.
Skipper: Horse Lovin' (previous Western) - $22.00.
Todd: Ken's friend. $18.00.
Tracey: Barbie's friend. $18.00.
Barbie and Friends Pack: Includes P.J. and Ken. $95.00.

1984:
Ken: Crystal - $22.00. Great Shape - $18.00. Sun Gold Malibu - $20.00.

P.J.: Sun Gold Malibu - $20.00. Sweet Roses - $22.00.

Skipper: Great Shape - $18.00. Sun Gold Malibu - $20.00.

1985

Ken: Day to Night - $30.00. Sun Gold (black) - $20.00.

Skipper: Hot Stuff - $22.00.

1986

Ken: Sun Lovin' Malibu - $20.00. Dream Glow (black) - $28.00. Tropical (black or white) - $18.00.

Miko: Tropical - $30.00.

Skipper: Tropical - $18.00.

1987

Ken: Jewels Secret (black or white) - $25.00.

Skipper: Jewels Secret - $20.00.

Whitney: Jewels Secret - $30.00.

1988

Ken: Perfume Giving (black or white) - $25.00. California Dream - $20.00.

Bobsy: Sensations doll. $25.00.

Belinda: Sensations doll. $25.00.

Becky: Sensations doll. $25.00.

Christie: Island Fun - $20.00. California Dreams - $25.00.

Miko: Island Fun - $25.00.

Midge: California Dream - $30.00.

12" ALL-STAR KEN with molded side-parted hair. Made in Mexico in 1989. $20.00. *Courtesy Kathy Tvrdik.*

11½" ALL-STAR MIDGE with freckles and green eyes. Made in Malaysia in 1989. $15.00. *Courtesy Kathy Tvrdik.*

Skipper: Island Fun - $20.00. Teen Sweetheart - $25.00. Party Teen - $25.00. Cheerleader Teen - $30.00. Workout Teen - $18.00.

Steven: Island Fun - $30.00.

Theresa: Island Fun - $30.00. California Dream - $25.00.

Whitney: Perfume Pretty - $25.00.

1989

Ken: Super Star - $15.00. Super Star (black) - $15.00. Beach Blast - $15.00. Animal Lovin' - $18.00. Dance Club - $20.00. My First - $15.00. Cool Times - $15.00.

Christie: Beach Blast - $18.00. Style Magic - $20.00. Cool Times - $18.00.

Courtney: Teentime - $20.00.

Devon: Dance Club - $20.00.

Kayla: Dance Club - $20.00.

Nikki: Animal Lovin' - $22.00.

Midge: Cool Times - $20.00.

Miko: Beach Blast - $20.00.

Skipper: Beach Blast - $20.00. Teentime - $22.00. Homecoming Queen - $28.00. Homecoming Queen (black) - $28.00.

Steven: Beach Blast - $20.00.

Theresa: Beach Blast - $20.00. Cool Times - $20.00.

Whitney: Style Magic - $22.00.

12" NOW LOOK KEN with long rooted hair that is side parted. Has open/closed smiling mouth and heavy painted eyebrows. Formal outfit sold through Montgomery Wards in 1976. $60.00. *Courtesy Renie Culp.*

THE SUN SET MALIBU KEN is from 1970 and SUN GOLD MALIBU KEN is from 1983. Each - $20.00. *Courtesy Gloria Anderson.*

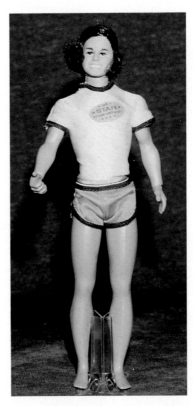

12" SPORT & SHAVE KEN from 1980. Marked "Mattel, Inc." on head and "Mattel, Inc./1966/Taiwan" on body. $18.00. *Courtesy Renie Culp.*

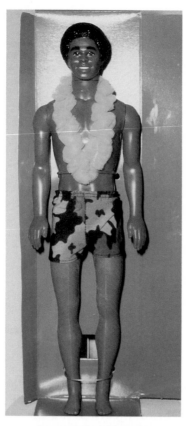

TROPICAL KEN from 1985. $20.00. *Courtesy Kathy Tvrdik.*

12" KEN ROCKER with rooted hair and long silver coat. Made in Taiwan. From 1986. $65.00. *Courtesy Kathy Tvrdik.*

From the WEDDING DAY SET, 12" ALAN GROOM (left) and KEN BEST MAN (right) are dressed for the marriage of ALAN and MIDGE. ALAN was made in China; KEN in Malaysia. From 1989–1990. ALAN - $75.00; KEN - $65.00. *Courtesy Kathy Tvrdik.*

11½" JAZZIE and 12" DUDE from the JAZZIE series. She has bendable knees. He has molded highlighted hair. Other dolls in the series are CHELSIE and STACIE. Made in Malaysia in 1988. JAZZIE - $35.00. DUDE - $30.00. *Courtesy Kathy Tvrdik.*

11½" FRANCIE with long inset lashes, bendable knees, and jointed waist. From 1967. $85.00 up. *Courtesy Kathy Tvrdik.*

11½" FRANCIE in original box has a twist 'n turn waist. Doll out of box is GROWING PRETTY HAIR FRANCIE. Both have brown eyes and long inset lashes. Each - $95.00. *Courtesy Gloria Anderson.*

TRULY SCRUMPTIOUS in two outfits from the movie *Chitty Chitty Bang Bang.* Made in 1968–1969. Each - $250.00 up. *Courtesy Margaret Mandel.*

One of the sets of YOUNG SWEETHEARTS by Mattel in 1975. These are MELINDA and MICHAEL. Both are original but missing shoes. Both are action figures with extra joints. Each - $40.00.

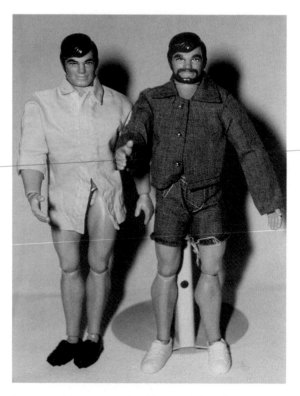

Both are BIG JIM made by Mattel. They have molded-on torso undergarments. One with beard has button in back that activates chopping motion in arm. Marked "1971." Each - $45.00. *Courtesy Kathy Tvrdik.*

Mint in box CHATTY CATHY with sleep eyes, rooted hair, and two front teeth. (Teeth are often missing.) Made of plastic and vinyl. MIB - $185.00. Doll alone - $65.00. *Courtesy Jeannie Mauldin.*

20" CHATTY CATHY dolls with brunette hair. One has blues eyes; the other has brown. Doll on right shown without white eyelet dress top and slip. Also she has replaced shoes and socks. Both are marked "Chatty Cathy/Patent Pending MCMLX (1960)/by Mattel, Inc. Hawthorne, Calif." Mint condition - $65.00; played with - $40.00. Brown eyes - $70.00. *Courtesy Kathy Tvrdik.*

18" BEANY AND CECIL, THE SEASICK SEA SERPENT were characters from TV cartoon show. BEANY has cloth body and vinyl head, hands, and feet. Cap with propeller is also vinyl. CECIL is plush and also came in 14" size. Mint in box - $60.00. Doll alone - $30.00. Cecil alone - $20.00. *Courtesy Jeannie Mauldin.*

22" TALKING MRS. BEASLEY from TV show "Family Affair." Cloth with vinyl face and plastic glasses. Removable collar and skirt. Pull string talker. Made in 1967 to 1974. $70.00. *Courtesy Kathy Tvrdik.*

18" BUGS BUNNY pull string talker made of cloth and vinyl. Marked "Warner Bros., Inc." on head. Tagged "1971/Warner Bros. Inc./Mattel, Inc." (There is also a 19" plush with vinyl face and pull string. It is marked "Mattel/Bugs Bunny Warner Bros. Pict., Inc. 1969.") $48.00. *Courtesy Kathy Tvrdik.*

21" LINUS THE LIONHEARTED pull string talker from 1966–1967. Corduroy with felt mane and vinyl face. Has crown crest with name on his belly. $48.00. *Courtesy Jeannie Mauldin.*

17" TEACHY KEEN is a pull string talker with painted features and vinyl head. Body and limbs are cloth. This pre-school doll has buttons, zipper, pockets, snaps, and shoe laces to teach motor skills. Has red plastic purse on arm. All original and mint. $30.00 up. *Courtesy Jeannie Mauldin.*

2" all vinyl LAFFY LEMON KOLA KIDDLE with painted features. Original. From 1967. $20.00.

VIOLET KOLOGNE came inside a cologne bottle and was part of a nine doll set. LILY OF VALLEY had white hair; APPLE BLOSSOM, green; ROSEBUD, red; HONEY-SUCKLE, yellow, SWEET PEA, yellow; BLUE BELL, blue; GARDENIA, white; ORANGE BLOSSOM, orange. Made 1968–1969. $20.00. *Courtesy Kathy Tvrdik.*

3½" LADY CRIMSON TEA PARTY KIDDLE. There are four in set, and each came with a different design cup and saucer. LADY LACE has white lace ballgown, blonde sausage curls on sides of head, and gold/blue design on tea set. LADY LAVENDER has lavender ballgown, blonde hair, and lavender/pink set. LADY SILVER has blue ballgown, brown hair, and blue/purple design. Mint in package - $100.00.

2" SWEET TREATS SPOONFULS doll made by Mattel in 1979. This one is PEACHIE PARFAIT with orange hair and came in blue or lime green spoon. $8.00. *Courtesy Kathy Tvrdik.*

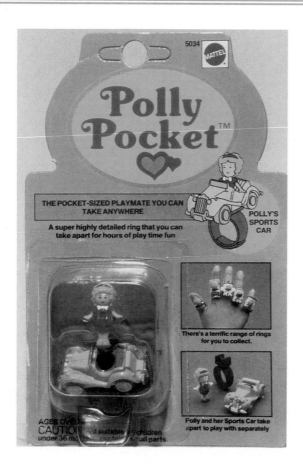

1½" POLLY POCKET in bubble pack with different play items. Snap POLLY into car for separate play or onto ring to wear. Others included bed and bath tub. Made by Mattel in 1990. $6.00. *Courtesy Kathy Tvrdik.*

4" DRESSY has one-piece body and limbs and large plastic head. Pull string talker when head is pulled up. As head returns to body, it says "Here comes my body" and "I've lost my head over you." Came in all hair colors and different clothes. Face has paper sticker features. Marked "Mattel" and made in 1971. $16.00. *Courtesy Gloria Anderson.*

7½" multi-jointed villians from TV cartoon show, "Bravestarr." (It had a futuristic wild west theme.) Top left is TEX HEX, top right is HANDLEBAR, and bottom right is SANDSTORM. All figures in the series are made of rigid vinyl and have a lever in their backs that operates their arms. Each - $15.00. *Courtesy Don Tvrdik.*

19" HOT LOOKS doll named STACEY. Vinyl head with stockinette body. Note how body and underwear are sewn together. Very posable. Made in 1986. Mint in box - $65.00. Nudes - $35.00 each. *Courtesy Pat Graff (left photo) and private collection (right photo).*

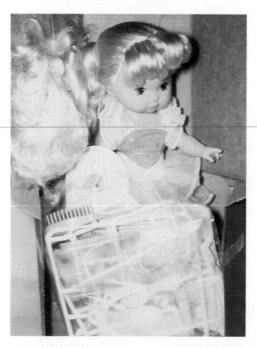

7" WEE LIL' MISS BALLERINA made of vinyl with painted features. Has heart painted on cheek. There are a number of LIL' MISS dolls such as LIL' MISS MAGIC HAIR and LIL' MISS MAKEUP. Also came in 13" size. From 1990. $12.00. *Courtesy Kathy Tvrdik.*

11" DANCING PRETTY BALLERINA has key wound mechanism for dancing. Has painted eyes and smile. Rooted hair is piled high on head. First on market in 1990. Made in China. $20.00. *Courtesy Kathy Tvrdik.*

11" M.C. HAMMER is an excellent personality figure. Made of plastic and vinyl and is multi-jointed. Comes with cassette message and glasses. Marked "Mattel 1991." $35.00. *Courtesy Kathy Tvrdik.*

7–8" WIZARD OF OZ set made by Mego. All are multi-jointed action figures. Marked on backs "MCMLXXII (1972)/Pat. Pending/Made in Hong Kong" and "M.G.M., Inc." Heads marked "1975 Mego, Inc." Each - $10.00–20.00. *Courtesy Sheila Stephenson.*

Shown are 12½" and 8" dolls of TV's "Charlie's Angels" – FARRAH FAWCETT-MAJORS, JACLYN SMITH, CHERYL LADD, and KATE JACKSON. The smaller dolls are multi-jointed and have bendable knees. All are original. From 1974–1975. 8" - $12.00; 12½" - $20.00. *Courtesy David Spurgeon.*

Characters from TV show, "Love Boat." Left photo: 5" DOC, ISSAC, and GOPHER. Right photo: 5" JULIE and 3½" VICKI. All are made of all rigid vinyl with jointed neck, shoulders, and hips. Molded-on clothes. Marked "1981/Mego Corp./Aaron Spelling Productions." Each - $9.00. *Courtesy Kathy Tvrdik.*

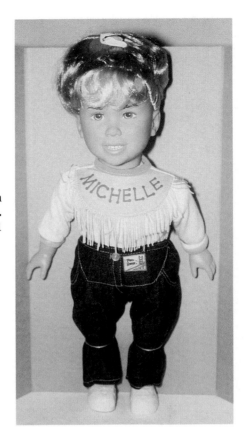

15" MICHELLE, from TV show "Full House," is a pull string talker. Has cloth body and upper limbs. Head, hands, and feet are vinyl. Marked "1991 Meritus Ind." $40.00. *Courtesy Kathy Tvrdik.*

～ Mollye ～

Mollye Goldman of Mollye International did not have a factory to make dolls. Like many doll companies during this period, she purchased dolls from other sources and dressed them herself. Goldman was a fashion clothes designer by vocation, but she chose to create doll clothes. As a designer, she worked for American Character, Arranbee, Junel, Joy, and Royal International. For some companies, such as Horsman and Ideal, she served both as designer and manufacturer of their doll clothing. Because other doll companies dressed blank, unmarked dolls and marketed them with only a paper wrist tag, it can be a challenge to properly identify a Mollye doll.

18" all hard plastic BRIDE made by Mollye International in 1953. Wearing beautiful wedding gown with one wide row of lace at hem. Has open mouth and glued-on styled wig. $300.00 up. *Courtesy Jeannie Nespoli.*

18" all hard plastic PEGGY ROSE BRIDE from 1957. (Mollye had dressed other PEGGY ROSE dolls earlier, and they were made of composition.) Has glued-on saran wig. Gown and capped veil are original. This gown is very similar to a gown designed by Mollye for American Character's SWEET SUE. Mollye's design "signature" is an oversized bonnet. $300.00 up. *Courtesy Kris Lundquist.*

17–18" DEBBIE BRIDE from 1955. Made of top quality hard plastic. Has mohair wig, eyeshadow above eyes, and open mouth. Dressed and sold by Mollye International. Missing collar veil (wide brim hat lace matches collar lace) with short net veil. $300.00 up. *Courtesy Kathy Tvrdik.*

14" all hard plastic SHARA LOU has turned-up nose, sleep eyes, molded eyelids, and mohair wig. Purchased by Mollye as blank to be dressed. Sold by her in 1954. Wearing knee length day dress. $285.00 up. *Courtesy Kris Lundquist.*

Close-up of one of the PEGGY ROSE hard plastic dolls purchased as a "blank" from another dollmaking firm. She was then dressed and marketed under the name Mollye Internationals. She has on a ballgown. From 1957. $300.00 up. *Courtesy Kris Lundquist.*

⌒ Monica Studios ⌒

The Monica Studios were located in Hollywood, California, and Mrs. Hansi Share created the doll with human hair embedded in its scalp so it could be combed and styled. The first dolls were 20–24" tall and made in 1941. In 1942, Moncia dolls were 17" tall and called Veronica, Rosalind, and Joan. In 1943, the sizes changed to 17" and 20" tall with 36 different oufits available. Those sizes stayed the same in 1944, but there were only 24 outfits marketed. The hard plastic era began at this time, but Monica did not make any dolls in that medium until 1949. The first hard plastic doll was named Marion. Hair was also embedded into the scalp the the hard plastic dolls. The last evidence that the company was still in business was in 1951. To read the history of the company, see *Modern Collector's Dolls, Series 2*, on page 273.

21" MONICA doll made of all composition. Hair is rooted into scalp. All original and mint only because of the restoration techniques of Peggy Millhouse. This doll's clothes were extremely soiled with shelf grease and dirt. In this condtion - $900.00. *Courtesy Peggy Millhouse.*

Left: 17" MONICA made of all composition with human hair wig embedded into scalp. Original and in mint condition. In this condition - $700.00. *Courtesy Jeannie Nespoli.*

✑ Naber Kids ✑

Collecting is a hobby – time well spent in relaxation and amusement. Naber Kids, created by Harold Naber, exhibit this facet of amusement in doll collecting. Each doll has its own fun personality and character. The following doll list and values are from the "Naberhood News," a very important newsletter for anyone interested in Naber Kids. Its mailing address is 8915 South Suncoast Blvd., Homosassa, Florida, 34446.

Item No.	Name	Type	Year	Status	Limitation	Issue Price	Current Values
2071	Milli Molli Frog L., urethane hands and feet	Eskimo doll	1984	retired	less than 300	$36.00	unknown
2072	Billy Molli Frog L., urethane hands and feet	Eskimo doll	1984	retired	less than 100	$36.00	unknown
2073	Chestnut kind	Eskimo doll	1984	retired	less than 50	$36.00	unknown
3001	Molli (first Naber Kid) carved in Alaska	Naber Kids	1984	retired	1001 days	$36.00	$1,000.00 up
3002	Jake (second Naber Kid) carved in Alaska	Naber Kids	1985	retired	1001 days	$36.00	$1,300.00 up
3003	Max (third Naber Kid) carved in Alaska	Naber Kids	1985	retired	1001 days	$36.00	$1,100.00 up
3004	Ashley (fourth Naber Kid) carved in Florida	Naber Kids	1986	retired	1001 days	$59.00	$775.00
3005	Milli (fifth Naber Kid) carved in Florida	Naber Kids	1986	retired	1001 days	$59.00	$575.00
3006	Maurice (sixth Naber Kid) carved in Florida	Naber Kids	1987	retired	1001 days	$69.00	$800.00 up
3007	Maxine (seventh Naber Kid) carved in Maine	Naber Kids	1987	retired	1001 days	$69.00	$400.00
3008	Sissi (eighth Naber Kid) carved in Georgia	Naber Kids	1988	retired	1001 days	$90.00	$750.00
3009	Frieda (ninth Naber Kid) carved in Georgia	Naber Kids	1988	retired	1001 days	$90.00	$600.00
3010	Walter (tenth Naber Kid) carved in Florida	Naber Kids	1988	retired	1001 days	$90.00	$475.00
3011	Peter (11th Naber Kid) carved in Arizona	Naber Kids	1988	retired	1001 days	$90.00	$425.00
3012	Pam (12th Naber Kid) carved in Arizona	Naber Kids	1988	retired	1001 days	$90.00	$465.00
3013	Darina (13th Naber Kid) carved in Florida	Naber Kids	1988	retired	1001 days	$90.00	$500.00
3014	Sami (14th Naber Kid) carved in Arizona	Naber Kids	1989	retired	1001 days	$123.00	$300.00
3015	Samantha (15th Naber Kid) carved in Arizona	Naber Kids	1989	retired	1001 days	$123.00	$365.00
3016	Freddi (16th Naber Kid) carved in Arizona	Naber Kids	1989	retired	1001 days	$123.00	$400.00
3017	Amy (17th Naber Kid) carved in Arizona	Naber Kids	1989	retired	1001 days	$123.00	$300.00
3018	Heidi (18th Naber Kid) carved in Germany	Naber Kids	1990	retired	1001 days	$150.00	$400.00
3019	Mishi (19th Naber Kid) carved in Germany	Naber Kids	1990	retired	1001 days	$150.00	$300.00

Item No.	Name	Type	Year	Status	Limitation	Issue Price	Current Values
3020	Hoey (20th Naber Kid) carved in Germany	Naber Kids	1990	retired	1001 days	$150.00	$300.00
3021	Paula (21th Naber Kid) carved in Germany	Naber Kids	1990	retired	1001 days	$150.00	$250.00
3022	Willi (22nd Naber Kid) carved in Germany	Naber Kids	1991	retired	1001 days	$180.00	$250.00
3023	Eric (23rd Naber Kid) carved in Germany	Naber Kids	1991	retired	1001 days	$180.00	$300.00
3024	Denise (24th Naber Kid) carved in Germany	Naber Kids	1991	available	1001 days	$180.00	$250.00
3025	Henry (25th Naber Kid) carved in Germany	Naber Kids	1991	retired	588 pcs. made	$200.00	$500.00 up
3026	Elsi (26th Naber Kid) carved in Germany	Naber Kids	1991	available	1001 days	$200.00	$275.00
3027	Benni (27th Naber Kid) carved in Germany	Naber Kids	1991	available	1001 days	$200.00	$300.00
3028	Sarah (28th Naber Kid) carved in Germany	Naber Kids	1991	available	1001 days	$200.00	$250.00
3029	Posi (29th Naber Kid) carved in Germany	Naber Kids	1991	available	1001 days	$200.00	$250.00
3030	Joseph (30th Naber Kid) carved in Germany	Naber Kids	1992	available	1001 days	$200.00	$265.00

19" ALICE was the first in the series of NEW GENERATION NABER KIDS. She is a delightful doll with extra joints at the waist, elbows, and knees. The shoes are carved on. Doll is extremely posable. $100.00 up.

Item No.	Name	Type	Year	Status	Limitation	Issue Price	Current Values
3031	Josi (31th Naber Kid) carved in Germany	Naber Kids	1992	available	1001 days	$200.00	$225.00
3032	Tony (32nd Naber Kid) carved in Germany	Naber Kids	1992	available	1001 days	$200.00	$285.00
3033	Phil (Special edition) for Neat Things, Indiana	Naber Kids	1992	retired	200 pcs. made	$220.00	unknown
3034	Juanita (34th Naber Kid) carved in Germany	Naber Kids	1992	available	1001 days	$200.00	$250.00
3035	Christina (35th Naber Kid) carved in Germany	Naber Kids	1992	available	1001 days	$200.00	$225.00
3036	Rita Witch (Special edition) for Baby Me, Massachusett	Naber Kids	1992	retired	200 pcs. made	$220.00	unknown
3037	Richie & Flink (Special edition) for Butcher's…, Michigan	Naber Kids	1992	retired	200 pcs. made	$275.00	unknown
3038	Marcie (38th Naber Kid) carved in Germany	Naber Kids	1992	available	1001 days	$200.00	$225.00
3100	Alice (New Generation– Naber Kids)	Naber Kids	1994	available	1001 pcs	$99.00	same
3101	Albert (New Generation– Naber Kids)	Naber Kids	1994	available	1001 pcs	$99.00	same
3102	Buk (New Generation– Naber Kids)	Naber Kids	1994	available	1001 pcs	$99.00	same
3103	Bubba (New Generation– Naber Kids)	Naber Kids	1994	available	1001 pcs	$99.00	same
3104	Clarissa (New Generation– Naber Kids)	Naber Kids	1994	available	1001 pcs	$99.00	same
4001	A. Schmalz protot. (light pink urethane)	Schmalz Orphan	1992	retired	24 made		unknown
4002	B. Schmalz protot. (light pink urethane)	Schmalz Orphan	1992	retired	15 made		unknown
4003	A. Schmalz porcel. (light & dark)	Schmalz Orphan	1992	retired	13 made		unknown
4004	A. Schmalz (fig.) (oak and walnut grain)	Schmalz Orphan	1992	retired	223 made	$88.00	same
4005	B. Schmalz (fig.) (oak and walnut grain)	Schmalz Orphan	1992	retired	114 made	$88.00	same
4006	C. Schmalz (fig.) (oak and walnut grain)	Schmalz Orphan	1992	retired	124 made	$88.00	same
4007	D. Schmalz (German oak, business suit)	Schmalz Orphan	1993	available	3,600 pcs.	$88.00	same
4008	E. Schmalz (cherry birch, little dress)	Schmalz Orphan	1993	available	3,600 pcs.	$88.00	same
4009	F. Schmalz (cherry birch, Bavarian boy)	Schmalz Orphan	1993	available	3,600 pcs.	$88.00	same
4010	G. Schmalz (sassafras) (bathrobe, shower cap)	Schmalz Orphan	1993	available	3,600 pcs.	$88.00	same
4011	H. Schmalz (cherry birch, flasher coat)	Schmalz Orphan	1993	available	3,600 pcs.	$88.00	same
4012	I. Schmalz (black walnut, Bavarian girl)	Schmalz Orphan	1993	available	3,600 pcs.	$88.00	same
5001	Adam	Wild Wood Baby	1993	retired	98 made	$220.00	$300.00

Item No.	Name	Type	Year	Status	Limitation	Issue Price	Current Values
5002	Brandy, 20"	Wild Wood Baby	1993	retired	99 made	$375.00	$450.00
5003	Clarence, 20"	Wild Wood Baby	1993	available	1001 pcs.	$220.00	same
5004	Dolly (1), 20"	Wild Wood Baby	1993	retired	136 made	$220.00	$250.00
5005	Dolly (2), 20"	Wild Wood Baby	1993	available	825 made	$220.00	same
5006	Erwin, 20"	Wild Wood Baby	1993	available	1001 pcs.	$220.00	same
5007	Felix (cow), 20"	Wild Wood Baby	1993	available	1001 pcs.	$220.00	same
5008	Gisela (dress), 20"	Wild Wood Baby	1993	available	1001 pcs.	$220.00	same
5009	Herbert, 20" (RR engineer)	Wild Wood Baby	1993	available	1001 pcs.	$220.00	same
5010	Iffi (Eskimo)	Wild Wood Baby	1993	available	1001 pcs.	$220.00	same
5011	Joe (cowboy)	Wild Wood Baby	1993	available	1001 pcs.	$220.00	same

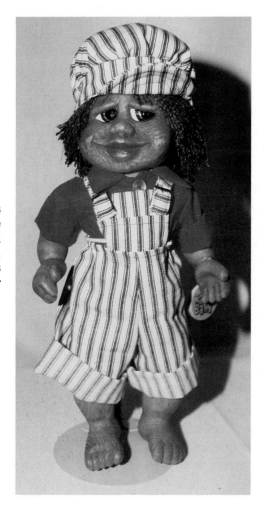

13" NABER BABY named BERNHARD from 1994. Has wooden and paper tags stating "Bernhard is my name and Naber Baby is my game." Made of resin with cloth joints at shoulders and hips. Hair is stripped burlap. BERNHARD represents a carpenter, and his expression is one of "happy-woe." Could it be his house fell down or he just hammered his thumb. $100.00.

Item No.	Name	Type	Year	Status	Limitation	Issue Price	Current Values
5012	Kaely (Mexican)	Wild Wood Baby	1993	available	1001 pcs.	$220.00	same
7001	Micki (representing the African continent)	Naber Gestalt	1993	available	101 pcs.	$1,500.00	same
7002	Iko (representing the European continent)	Naber Gestalt	1993	available	101 pcs.	$1,500.00	same
7003	Sung (representing the Asian continent)	Naber Gestalt	1993	available	101 pcs.	$1,500.00	same
10001	Alexander (convention) (baby pajamas w/blanket)	Naber Baby	1994	sold out	1001 pcs.	$99.00	unknown
10002	Bernahard (railroad engineer w/cap)	Naber Baby	1994	available	1001 pcs.	$99.00	same
10003	Horace (short pants, shirt, bowtie, hat)	Naber Baby	1994	available	1001 pcs.	$99.00	same
10004	Elizabeth (little dress w/blanket, booties)	Naber Baby	1994	available	1001 pcs.	$99.00	same
10005	Bernice (little dress, booties)	Naber Baby	1994	available	1001 pcs.	$99.00	same
10006	Ivan (Eskimo parka, pants, fur trim)	Naber Baby	1994	available	1001 pcs.	$99.00	same
10007	Natasha (Eskimo parka, pants, fur trim)	Naber Baby	1994	available	1001 pcs.	$99.00	same
10008	Eileen (Club Baby only)	Naber Baby	1994	Club only	200 pcs.	$99.00	unknown
10009	Kilo (Eskimo Baby) (Winter/summer parka)	Naber Baby	1994	available	1001 pcs.	$99.00	same

⇜ Nancy Ann Storybook Dolls ⇝

Muffie can be a great addition to any collection that includes hard plastic or 8" tall dolls. Her clothes were well made, and she has what Ginny and Ginger have going for them in that some of her clothes are tagged and there are booklets that show those clothes. Another plus for collectors is many doll books contain information on Muffie. There is one book specializing in this doll – *The Muffie Puzzle* written by Lillian Roth and Heather Browning Maciak. It is an excellent book for any serious collector. (For information about the book, contact the authors at 403 Euclid St., Santa Monica, California 90402-2127.)

All Muffies were made of hard plastic from 1953 to 1956. From 1956 until production end in 1960, the body and limbs remained hard plastic while the head became vinyl with rooted hair. Muffie was reintroduced in 1968 as a hard plastic walker dressed in international costumes.

Muffie was a strung doll in 1953 and 1954. There was also few straight leg walkers in 1954. Their production continued in 1955 and into part of 1956. The manufacturing of bend knee dolls began 1956.

In 1953 and 1954, Muffie had painted eyelashes over the eyes and no eyebrows. From 1955 to 1960, she had painted lashes over her eyes with painted eyebrows and small molded lashes.

Early clothes were untagged with attached slips and small plain brass snaps. Shoes were leatherette with center snaps. In 1955, the small brass snap was painted to match the oufit. At this same time, shoes became plastic with a side button closure. Shoes remained this way until production's end. In 1956, the plain clothes snaps were replaced by donut style gripper snaps and continued on clothes until 1960. From 1956 to 1960, the majority of the clothes were tagged.

The marks on Muffie were "Storybook Dolls/California" in 1953 through 1954. Beginning in 1955, the mark changed to "Storybook Dolls/California/Muffie."

When Muffie was reintroduced in 1968, she was an all hard plastic walker with a plastic walking mechanism instead of a metal one. The dolls were unmarked, and her clothes were international styles. Clothes snaps are the sewn-on types, and her shoes are plastic with one strap. There is a total of 250 outfits shown in brochures and at least 100 other authenic Muffie outfits. Clothes tags have a white background with blue print. They are imprinted "Styles by Nancy Ann Storybook Dolls, Inc. San Franciso."

BASIC MUFFIE with panties, shoes, and socks in red polka dot box. From 1953. $200.00. *Courtesy Maureen Fukushima.*

MUFFIE BALLERINA from 1953. Has painted lashes over eyes and no eyebrows. $300.00.
Courtesy Peggy Millhouse.

8" MUFFIE in oufit #609 "Margie" from 1953. All original. $250.00. *Courtesy Peggy Millhouse.*

Two strung MUFFIE dolls from 1953 (left) and 1954 (right). Both are dressed in #507 outfits. Doll in red dress has replaced shoes. The other is all original. 1953 - $225.00; 1954 - $250.00. *Courtesy Peggy Millhouse.*

Strung MUFFIE dressed in all original outfit #806-1954. $250.00. *Courtesy Peggy Pergande.*

Walker doll from 1955 with painted eyebrows. Dressed in outfit #708-1953. $250.00. *Courtesy Maureen Fukushima.*

1955 MUFFIE with eyebrows dressed in 1954 outfit. She seems to be original. $250.00. *Courtesy Susan Giradot.*

Rare bald headed MUFFIE that was also used as a groom. Has sprayed blonde hair and dressed in original Roy Rogers cowboy suit. (Grooms have black painted hair.) $375.00 up. *Courtesy Maureen Fukushima.*

Strung MUFFIE in Storybook style outfit #814-1953. Marked "Storybook Dolls/California/Muffie." $300.00.

Courtesy Maureen Fukushima.

MUFFIE in outfit #803-1954. All original. $250.00.

Courtesy Susan Giradot.

8" MUFFIE dolls with painted eyelashes and mohair wigs. Both are strung and marked "Storybook Dolls Calif." Both were purchased from San Francisco department store in 1950s and have original price tags. White dotted dress is $3.45 and party dress is $3.98. Each - $250.00. *Courtesy Glorya Woods.*

MUFFIE from 1955 with a 1953 #504 "Darling Margie" outfit. $250.00. *Courtesy Peggy Millhouse.*

"Muffie's Favorite Fashions" is the name of this #602-1954 outfit. Doll is walker and unmarked. $175.00. *Courtesy Maureen Fukushima.*

MUFFIE dressed in #811-1954 outfit "Muffie Special Occasions Styles." Walker doll with painted eyebrows. $175.00. *Courtesy Maureen Fukushima.*

MUFFIE WALKER with painted eyebrows and green hair. Doll and outfit from 1955. $250.00. *Courtesy Maureen Fukushima.*

1955 MUFFIE dressed in outfit #704 "Dress Up Styles" from 1954. $175.00. *Courtesy Maureen Fukushima.*

"Muffie Rollerskater" from 1955. $225.00. *Courtesy Maureen Fukushima.*

MUFFIE shown in #501-1955 with variation of print. All original except replaced hair braid ribbons. $175.00 *Courtesy Maureen Fukushima.*

All original MUFFIE doll with molded eyelashes. She is also one of the later strung straight leg dolls. The outfit is #708-1955. $200.00. *Courtesy Peggy Pergande.*

MUFFIE BRIDE AND GROOM are walker dolls that have painted eyebrows. Her gown is #900-3 from 1956. Both are marked on back "Storybook Dolls/Calif./Muffie. Bride - $175.00; groom - $200.00. *Courtesy Maureen Fukushima.*

1955 MUFFIE with painted eyebrows. This skirt and top outfit uses the same material as dress outfit #605-1955. $175.00. *Courtesy Maureen Fukushima.*

MUFFIE dressed in all original outfit #706-3. From 1956. $175.00. *Courtesy Maureen Fukushima.*

MUFFIE dressed in outfit #651-3, "Pinafore Style" from 1956. $175.00. *Courtesy Maureen Fukushima.*

This really cute MUFFIE is from 1956 and in mint condition. There is a "donut" snap in back exactly like one on belt. She has red, white, and blue flowers around brim of hat. $225.00. *Courtesy Maureen Fukushima.*

This MUFFIE in mint condition shows the pin joints in the bend knees. From 1956. $150.00. *Courtesy Maureen Fukushima.*

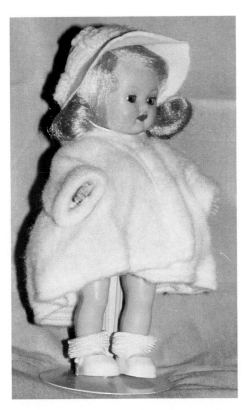

MUFFIE WALKER with painted eyebrows from 1956. Wearing fleece coat with matching felt and fleece hat. $150.00. *Courtesy Maureen Fukushima.*

A cute MUFFIE dressed in a very attractive, but unknown, outfit. $200.00. *Courtesy Maureen Fukushima.*

Fully marked MUFFIE dressed in original unknown outfit from 1957. $175.00. *Courtesy Maureen Fukushima.*

7½" MUFFIE of the International Series. She is one of the all hard plastic, reintroduced dolls. Has sleep eyes and is all original. Unmarked. $95.00. *Courtesy Margaret Mandel.*

10" DEBBIE and 8" MUFFIE dressed alike in adorable outfits. From 1955. Muffie - $250.00. Debbie - $165.00.
Courtesy Maureen Fukushima.

DEBBIE and MUFFIE from 1955. Both are all hard plastic. Debbie has bend knees. Muffie - $200.00. Debbie - $125.00. *Courtesy Maureen Fukushima.*

10" all original DEBBIE dressed in outfit #603-D-1955. There is a matching dress for MUFFIE. She is a bend knee walker. $165.00. *Courtesy Maureen Fukushima.*

All original DEBBIE dressed in cowgirl outfit with Miss America banner. Holster carries blue plastic gun. From 1955. $225.00. *Courtesy Maureen Fukushima.*

4¾–5⅛" painted bisque NANCY ANN STORYBOOK dolls dressed in costumes. Each have jointed hips. Left: DUTCH with molded, painted socks. Center: QUAKER with painted socks and molded bangs. Right: Pudgy MEXICO in native costume. All dolls are original and in mint condition. Each - $200.00–275.00. *Courtesy Margaret Mandel.*

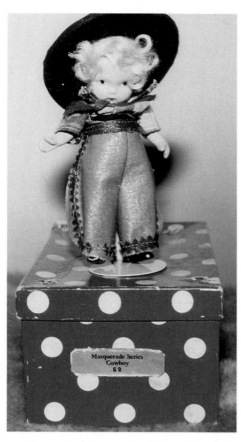

5½" painted bisque NANCY ANN STORYBOOK doll with jointed hips and painted-on socks. This one is #62 "Cowboy" from the Masquerade Series. $750.00 up. *Courtesy Susan Giradot.*

NANCY ANN STYLE SHOW DOLL called GINA BRIDE. Made of all hard plastic. Clothes are extremely well made. Doll is unmarked. $500.00 up. *Courtesy Jeannie Nespoli.*

All original NANCY ANN STYLE SHOW DOLL made of hard plastic. Missing silver paper arm tag with her name. $500.00 up. *Courtesy Jeannie Nespoli.*

NANCY ANN STYLE SHOW DOLL called BREATH OF SPRING. Made of all hard plastic and all original. Unmarked. Mint condition - $500.00 up. *Courtesy Jeannie Nespoli.*

NANCY ANN STYLE SHOW DOLL called GARDEN PARTY. Original and in mint condition. $500.00 up. *Courtesy Jeannie Nespoli.*

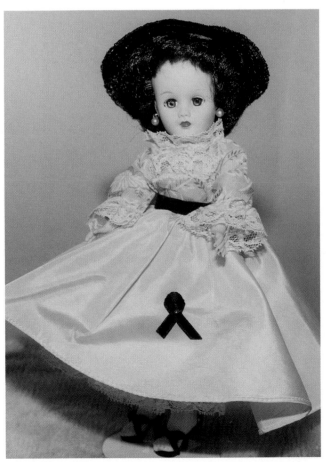

10½" MISS NANCY ANN is also called MARGIE ANN. All vinyl with sleep eyes and high heel feet. Original and in mint condtion. Marked "Miss Nancy Ann" on head. $125.00. *Courtesy Susan Giradot.*

13" LEONARDO from the TEENAGE MUTANT NINJA TURTLES was made by Playmates in 1991. Others in series are DONATELLO, RAPHAEL, and MICHAELANGELO. Their initials are on their belts. $40.00. *Courtesy Don Tvrdik.*

13" ROCKSTEADY, enemy of the TEENAGE MUTANT NINJA TURTLES. Other foes were BEBOP and SHREDDER. $40.00. *Courtesy Don Tvrdik.*

The evil KRANG is from the TEENAGE MUTANT NINJA TURTLES series. He is a small brain being from another dimension. Uses an android body for mobility and controls it from the torso. Marked "1991/Mirage Studio/ Playmates Toys." $40.00. *Courtesy Don Tvrdik.*

WATER BABY was made by Playmates in 1991. Vinyl doll fills with warm water for cuddling. She has beautiful molded yellow hair and painted eyes. All original. $32.00. *Courtesy Jeannie Mauldin.*

Left to right: 17" LUCY and 18" RICKY made of porcelain and cloth. Made in 1990–1991 by Hamilton Collection. 16½" RICKY, 14½" LUCY, 14½" ETHEL, and 15½" FRED made by Presents Dolls. Marked "1988 CBS Inc. Made in China." 15" LUCY with top hat was made by Effanbee in 1985. Hamilton Collection dolls - $95.00 each. Presents dolls - $75.00 each. Effanbee doll - $50.00. *Courtesy David Spurgeon.*

15" THREE STOOGES – LARRY, CURLY, AND MOE. Made by Presents and marked "1988 Herman Maurer Prod. Columbia." Current version of these dolls are 11–12" tall and made by Presents. Each - $26.00. *Courtesy David Spurgeon.*

THE MUNSTERS were marketed in late 1980s by Presents. Left to right: 11½" GRANDPA, 13" HERMAN, 9" EDDY, and 10½" LILY. (There was also a 13" Eddy.) Marked "1964 Kayro/VVE Prducts." Each - $26.00. *Courtesy David Spurgeon.*

⇐ Raggedy Ann & Andy ⇒

The very first Raggedy dolls were made by Johnny Gruelle and will be marked with a patent date.

Volland Company made the Raggedy dolls from 1920 to 1934. The eyelashes are low on the cheeks, and the feet turn outward. Some have oversized hands with free standing thumbs. They can have brown yarn hair and a long thin nose.

Georgene Averill made the dolls during the mid-1930s. Most have black outlined noses and will have a label sewn to body seam.

Knickerbocker made these Raggedy dolls from 1963 to 1982 when the company ended toy production.

Mollye also made these dolls. They were marked with name signed across the chest or with "Mollye International."

These 15" original RAGGEDY ANN & ANDY dolls are very worn from love and play. Made in the 1920s by Volland. In excellent condition - $1,700.00; fair condition - $600.00. *Courtesy Ellen Dodge.*

18" RAGGEDY ANN & ANDY dolls made by Georgene Averill. All are original. RAGGEDY ANN in the middle has unusual blue striped legs. Each - $700.00 up.
Courtesy Ellen Dodge.

AWAKE-ASLEEP RAGGEDY ANN & ANDY made by Georgene Averill. She is original; he is redressed. Each - $450.00 up. *Courtesy Ellen Dodge.*

RAGGEDY ANN & ANDY adventure books published in the 1920s and 1930s. "Marcella" was the name of Johnny Gruelle's daughter. He made up the rag doll characters and their stories to entertain her. Each book - $90.00 up.

Courtesy Ellen Dodge.

RAGGEDY ANN & ANDY made by Knickerbocker. Shown with dog, ARTHUR, which is hard to find. Dolls - $185.00 each. Dog - $70.00. *Courtesy Susan Giradot.*

⮜ Remco ⮞

The Littlechap Family was introduced by Remco in 1964. The represented upper middle class America. The father, John, is a doctor and "member of Lanesville Medical Society, former flight surgeon in United States Air Force, and loves his family and golf." He resembles Robert Young from "Father Knows Best." His wife, Lisa Littlechap, has an up-swept hairdo that has a strand of gray hair running through it. She is "a former model, wonderful cook, president of P.T.A., and best dressed woman in town."

The Littlechaps have two daughters. The oldest is Judy, "age 17, honor student at Lanesville High, loves parties and crazy desserts." The younger girl is Libby who is age 10 and "in the fifth grade, loves to climb trees, pester her sister and wants to be a doctor like her father."

The Littlechap Family did not sell well because they were awkward. Their legs were spread apart, which was to help them stand by themselves. Also the tilt of their heads, especially on Libby, was cumbersome.

JUDY LITTLECHAP is dressed for a football game, wearing a black V-neck pullover sweater, plaid tapper slacks, matching plaid scarf, and corduroy car coat. $45.00 up.

THE LITTLECHAP FAMILY, from left to right: the father, JOHN, dressed in his doctor's outfit, mother LISA wears two-piece V-neck dress with scarf and fur trimmed coat, daughter JUDY wears her high school dance dress (yellow wrist length jacket missing), and younger daughter LIBBY dressed to climb trees and play. Set - $300.00 up.

Richwood

Sandra Sue was made from the late 1940s to the late 1950s by the Richwood Enterprises Company of Annapolis, Maryland. Advertisements for the doll can be found in family style magazines that sell at the grocery stores, and she was offered for sale by Richwood as well as the few existing doll shops of her day.

During the first five to six years of Sandra Sue's life, the most purchased dolls were made by such companies as Dutchess Doll, Dolls Parts, Plated Moulds, Marcie, and dozens of others. These dolls are now referred to as "dime dolls" because many of them were "dress yourself" types and were sold in five & dime stores. Dressed with stapled-on clothes, dolls from these firms were also sold through Montgomery Wards and Sears & Roebucks. In the early years of collecting, Sandra Sue was passed over as being "just one of *those* dolls." She was sold heavily in the Eastern States but was not nationally distributed. Few ever made it past the Mississippi River.

Sandra Sue falls into this category, but she had more "class" and was more expensive than the standard dime doll. She had molded eyelids, high arched eyebrows, painted lashes below the eyes, and a saran wig. She also had the thin face look of the other dolls her size.

The cheaper dolls had a one-piece body and legs. (Some were jointed at the hips.) Sandra Sue had joints at the neck, shoulders, and hip. She is a walker but her head does not turn. The body and limbs are thin with good detail to the hands. All the fingers are molded together with the palms facing body.

The first Sandra Sue dolls had a built-in soles on the bottom of her flat feet with no toe detail. The second dolls had nice toe detail and flat feet. The third version had high heel feet. She had flat feet from 1949 to 1958, and high heel feet from 1958 to 1960.

The wardrobe for Sandra Sue would be the envy of all the other dolls in her small world. The quality of Sandra Sue herself was excellent, even if she does have the "second cousin" look of those dime dolls.

Sandra Sue also had the finest furniture ever created for a doll. The quality is exactly as one would want in their own home. The furniture had Duncan Phyfe styling and was made of solid wood. The manufacturer who designed this doll furniture also made furnishings for historical colonial homes. Although scaled for an 8" doll, the furniture is large. There is a 12" long four poster bed and a 12" tall solid mahogany wardrobe with a shelf for hats. Furniture pieces have brass handles and working parts, such as bureau drawers that opened and closed.

Cindy Lou is another doll marketed by Richwood. The dolls were purchased as blanks from another firm that made 14" dolls. She is an all hard plastic walker with a head that turns. She has sleep eyes and hair lashes and will be marked on her back "Made in U.S.A." inside a large circle. If found in the box, the top will have a clock with Cindy Lou's name running through it. It states "Around the Clock Fashions/Highland, Maryland."

Close-up of SANDRA SUE with painted lashes below eyes and molded lashes over eyes. *Courtesy Peggy Millhouse.*

225

A collection of SANDRA SUE dolls, all dressed differently. Each - $60.00–125.00. *Courtesy Peggy Millhouse.*

A high-heeled Sandra Sue in ball-gown. In mint condition. $150.00. *Courtesy Maureen Fukushima.*

Side view of 8" SANDRA SUE with her cute profile. Molded lashes over sleep eyes. Note "soles" of bare feet. $60.00. *Courtesy Mildred Lasky.*

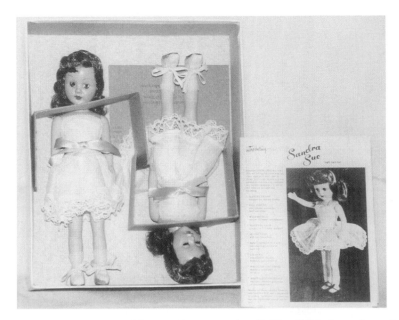

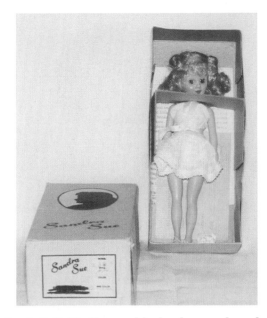

SANDRA SUE was sold as twins or pairs (left) which is unique in the doll field. She could also be purchased singly (right). The basic dolls came dressed in full slip and panties and wearing shoes and socks. Twins/pair - $215.00; single - $95.00. *Courtesy Maureen Fukushima.*

LITTLE WOMEN portrayed by SANDRA SUE dolls. There is also another doll in calf length, blue and white checked dress with long sleeves, lace cuffs, and a tiny ruffle near the hem. All are original. Each - $150.00. *Courtesy Maureen Fukushima.*

8" SANDRA SUE dressed in "Corornation Queen" outfit with beaded embroidery on gown. From 1953. $185.00. *Courtesy Maureen Fukushima.*

High-heeled SANDRA SUE dressed in cute "Going Shopping" outfit. Original. $95.00. *Courtesy Maureen Fukushima.*

High-heeled SANDRA SUE in formal wear with fur stole. $125.00. *Courtesy Maureen Fukushima.*

Very attractive "Majorette" outfit for SANDRA SUE. Included wooden baton. Hat is correct scale for doll but looks too tall. $125.00. *Courtesy Maureen Fukushima.*

High-heeled SANDRA SUE dressed in her Sunday best. Original. $95.00. *Courtesy Maureen Fukushima.*

Very pretty SANDRA SUE in original outfit. Made of all hard plastic with high-heeled feet. $90.00. *Courtesy Maureen Fukushima.*

High-heeled SANDRA SUE wearing felt coat and bonnet. Blue purse is also felt. Original shoes. $95.00. *Courtesy Maureen Fukushima.*

Flat-footed SANDRA SUE in Scottish style outfit. $95.00. *Courtesy Maureen Fukushima.*

Flat-footed SANDRA SUE in all original outfit. $95.00. *Courtesy Maureen Fukushima.*

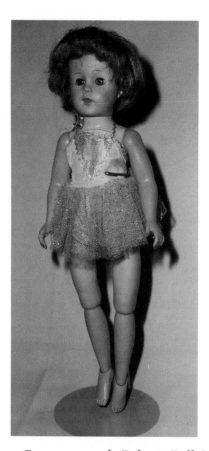

19" ROBERTA BALLERINA **made Roberta Doll Company. All hard plastic with vinyl head and arms. Extra joints at ankles and knees. Has sleep eyes and rooted hair. Marked "34." $60.00.** *Courtesy Kathy Tvrdik.*

20" TOBY BALLERINA **made by Roberta Doll Co. Has plastic body with vinyl head and arms. Sleep eyes with eyeshadow. Has key wind music box in head. Mark "20" on head. $45.00.** *Courtesy Carmen Moxley.*

⁓ Sasha ⁓

There has been a missing chapter to the Sasha story. It stems from the time Sasha Morgenthaler started to let other companies make the dolls for her. The first such company was Gotz of Germany who produced them from 1965 to 1969. The faces are painted slightly different, and the vinyl used is a little softer. The marks are an incised "Sasha Serie" in a circle on head and the same thing in three non-concentric circles on the back. From late 1969, the dolls were manufactured by Trenton Toys, Ltd. of Reddish, Stockbury, England, until 1986 when they went out of business. Most of the dolls are unmarked but will have a wrist tag. If the doll is marked, it is "Serie, England." All Sasha dolls are 16" tall.

Early SASHA **girl that came in a tube. (Top of tube made doll stand.) Original brunette with dark brown painted eyes. $325.00.** *Courtesy Shirley's Doll House.*

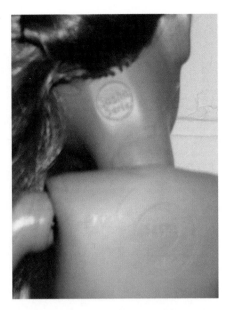

SASHA doll made by Gotz in 1965 to 1968. Original dress but has replaced leotards and shoes. Marked "Sasha Serie" in circle on head. Back has three non-concentric circles with "Sasha." $400.00 up.

Courtesy Pat Graff.

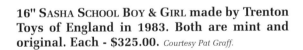

16" SASHA SCHOOL BOY & GIRL made by Trenton Toys of England in 1983. Both are mint and original. Each - $325.00. *Courtesy Pat Graff.*

16" SASHA boy and girl dolls, both black and white. Made in England and shipped in tubes. Tube tops became the doll stand. The black boy and girl are CALEB and CORA. The other boy is GREGOR. Each - $325.00. *Courtesy Ellen Dodge.*

20" doll made by Sayco in 1953. Has one-piece stuffed vinyl body with vinyl head, rooted hair, and sleep eyes. Has beautiful face color. Hair is in original set. All original. In this mint condition - $65.00. *Courtesy Pat Graff.*

9½" O.J. SIMPSON **action figure made by Shindana Toys in 1976. His full name is Orenthal James Simpson, and he was born in San Francisco on July 9, 1947. He was a running back for the Buffalo Bills from 1969 to 1977 and the San Francisco 49ers in 1978 and 1979. Value on this doll has wildly fluctuated from 1993 to 1995. Doll normally sold for about $85.00 but has been reportedly sold as high as $1,000.00!** *Courtesy Phyllis Kates.*

∽ Shirley Temple ∽

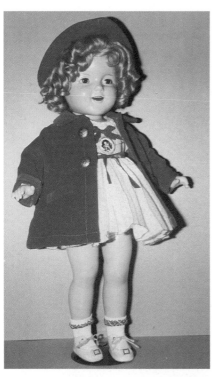

22" SHIRLEY TEMPLE dressed in velveteen coat and hat with two brass buttons on both. Coat set appeared in movie *Managed Money* of 1933. White organdy pleated dress with red pin dots has a rayon label. From *Curly Top* of 1935. Doll is marked on head and body. **$950.00 up.** *Courtesy Glorya Woods.*

13" SHIRLEY TEMPLE from movie *Our Little Girl* of 1935. Has two appliqued Scotty dogs on front of dress. Rayon label on dress. **$650.00.** *Courtesy Glorya Woods.*

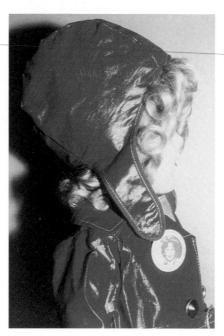

22" SHIRLEY TEMPLE in original avaiator outfit from the movie *Bright Eyes* of 1934. Imitation leather tagged jacket and helmet with white cotton N.R.A. tag, four brass buttons and buckle. Jacket and helmet are very rare. Wearing copy of overalls. **$1,000.00 up.** *Courtesy Glorya Woods.*

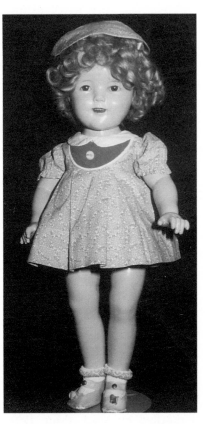

Beautiful example of 20" SHIRLEY TEMPLE dressed in sailor dress from 1936's *Poor Little Rich Girl.* This dress comes in various colors of blue. The old straw hat was added. In mint condition. **$950.00 up.** *Courtesy Martha Sweeney.*

20" SHIRLEY TEMPLE dressed in original outfit. The dress was commercially made and tagged "R.H. Macy & Co./New York." Doll is unmarked except for pink tag in her wig, "Ideal Novelty and Toy Co." **$800.00 up.** *Courtesy Martha Sweeney.*

18" and 20" CAPTAIN JANUARY dolls from 1936. White organdy dress with blue/white flowers, red heart-shaped buttons, and rayon label in front. 18" has flirty eyes. Both dolls are marked head and body. **18" - $750.00; 20" - $885.00.** *Courtesy Glorya Woods.*

18" OUR LITTLE GIRL from 1935. Dress has rayon label. Doll is marked on head and body. 6½" and 3¾" figurines are incised "Shirley" on base. **Doll - $725.00. Figurines - $95.00–125.00 each.** *Courtesy Glorya Woods.*

20" CAPTAIN JANUARY in original tagged linen dress with dotted Swiss yoke, puff sleeves, and inset front pleat. Doll marked on head. From 1936. $865.00.
Courtesy Glorya Woods.

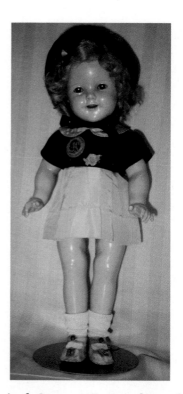

18" all original SHIRLEY TEMPLE dressed in tagged outfit. The color combination of dress (black or purple with yellow) comes from *Our Little Girl* of 1935. Marked on head. In mint condition. $875.00. *Courtesy Martha Sweeny.*

18" SHIRLEY TEMPLE may be from *Now and Forever* of 1934. Dress has eyelet lace in front and green cotton binding and lace trim. Fabric has a green, lavender, deep purple, and orange-red geometric design. Marked on head and body. $785.00. *Courtesy Margaret Mandel.*

13" SHIRLEY TEMPLE in rare bluebird print dress. (Pale aqua blue with white print) All original and in mint condition. In this dress - $725.00. *Courtesy Jo Keelen.*

16" CAPTAIN JANUARY doll in excellent condition. Wearing dress with smocked bodice and crimped pleated skirt. Has rayon dress tag. Her beautiful hair has not been disturbed except for flattening in back from laying in the box. All original and in mint condition. $725.00. *Courtesy Glorya Woods.*

16" CAPTAIN JANUARY from the school room scene. This photo shows the entire dress. $550.00. *Courtesy Marie Wolfe.*

SHIRLEY TEMPLE dolls in western outfits. Top left: 11" cowgirl. All original, including hat. Top right: 27" Ranger. Plaid shirt and hat added. Bottom left: 27" with darker chaps. Hat matches trim on chaps and vest. Bottom right: 25" Ranger with same outfit but different color vest and chap trim. 11" - $825.00; 25" - $1,200.00; 27" - $1,350.00. *Courtesy Jeannie Mauldin, Joanna Brunkin, Joan Amundson, Frasher Doll Auctions.*

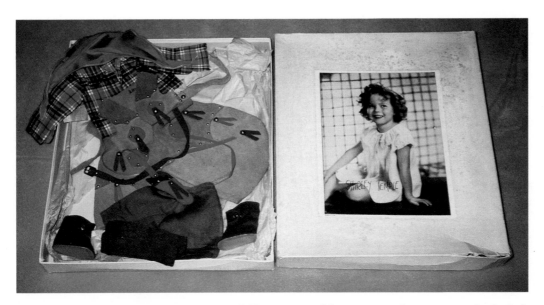

Ranger outfit for 18" SHIRLEY TEMPLE doll in original box. Note a hat was not included. Apparently only the dolls that came dressed in outfit had cowboy hats. In box - $185.00 up. *Courtesy Pat Sparks.*

Three SHIRLEY TEMPLE dolls that have pink tags inside wigs. Tags marked "Ideal Novelty and Toy Co." All wigs have bias tape around the edges. Center doll is 20" tall; the others are 18". Shown are BRIGHT EYES (left) with variation of plaid, BABY TAKES A BOW (center), and MERRILY YOURS with ruffle around skirt and blue ribbon added. 20" - $800.00; 18" - $700.00. *Courtesy Martha Sweeney.*

19" CURLY TOP from 1935. This dress can also be red with red and white striped collar. Doll marked on head. $765.00. *Courtesy Jo Keelen.*

Left to right: 22" CURLY TOP in sunburst dress from 1935. $925.00. 20" STAND UP & CHEER in polka dot dress from 1934. $865.00. 18" OUR LITTLE GIRL in Scotty dog dress from 1935. $725.00. 16" CURLY TOP in pin dot dress from 1935. $675.00. 13" BRIGHT EYES in plaid dress from 1934. $650.00. *Courtesy Glorya Woods.*

22" SHIRLEY TEMPLE dolls. Left to right: CURLY TOP in pin dot dress. CURLY TOP in sunburst dress. BABY TAKE A BOW in pink pleated dress. CURLY TOP in sunburst pleaded dress. STAND UP & CHEER in blue trimmed dress. Each - $925.00. *Courtesy Glorya Woods.*

18" SHIRLEY TEMPLE dolls. Left to right: BABY TAKES A BOW in blue pleated dress. BABY TAKES A BOW in red dotted dress. STAND UP & CHEER in red coin dot dress with red trim. OUR LITTLE GIRL in musical note dress. CURLY TOP in peach pleated print dress. Each - $725.00. *Courtesy Gloria Woods.*

13" CURLY TOP from 1935 with trunk and outfits. Includes roller skates with skate key and ice skates. Set - $1,200.00. *Courtesy Glorya Woods.*

13" SHIRLEY TEMPLE in rare bluebird dress with pink ribbon and button. (Another doll in this section wearing bluebird print has blue ribbon and button.) There is a plaid raincap and matching umbrella included. $1,100.00. *Courtesy Jeannie Vinner.*

Very rare SHIRLEY TEMPLE walker on chunky body. Has hard plastic body and rigid vinyl arms. Vinyl head has open/closed mouth with four teeth. All original and in mint condition with wrist tag and purse. Marked "Ideal Toy Corp./G-18" on back and "Ideal Toy Corp./ST-19-A" on head. $650.00 up. *Courtesy Jeannie Nespoli.*

All original 18" MARAMA from the 1940 movie, *Hurricane*. Made of all composition with black yarn/floss wig. Has painted eyes and teeth. Doll will be marked with size of doll and "Shirley Temple" on head and on back "U.S.A." and size of doll. $850.00.

Courtesy Idona Furnish.

15" SHIRLEY TEMPLE made of all composition with sleep eyes. On a toddler body (body cut at angle at hips). May be original. Marked "ST 5/0, CB" in circle "Germany." Very cute doll. $500.00. *Courtesy Martha Sweeney.*

12" SHIRLEY TEMPLE from 1957–1958. All vinyl with inset eyes and rooted hair. All original. $165.00.

Courtesy Kathy Tvrdik.

17" all vinyl SHIRLEY TEMPLE with rooted hair and sleep eyes. Original from 1959. $325.00. *Courtesy Susan Giradot.*

16½" SHIRLEY TEMPLE of the late 1950s. All vinyl with rooted hair and sleep eyes. The dress is most unusual. Although the dress style is original for this doll, the dress shown is a variation with three rows of trim at hem and trim around sleeves. All original with wrist tags. **$400.00.** *Courtesy Gloria Anderson.*

19" all vinyl SHIRLEY TEMPLE with rooted hair and flirty eyes. Wearing pink nylon dress with black velvet ribbon trim. Original pink butcher linen coat and bonnet are rare. Trimmed with lace and gripper snaps. Marked "Ideal Doll ST-19." **$450.00.** *Courtesy Margaret Mandel.*

8" SHIRLEY TEMPLE from 1982 set of reintroduced dolls. There were six dolls the first year: STAND UP AND CHEER (shown), HEIDI, THE LITTLEST REBEL, CAPTAIN JANUARY, and STOWAWAY. These same dolls came in 12" size also. Each - **$30.00.** *Courtesy Kathy Tvrdik.*

16½" SHIRLEY TEMPLE from 1974. Made of all vinyl with inset eyes and rooted hair. Considered to be one of the prettiest SHIRLEYS made. Marked "1972/Ideal Toy Corp./ST-14-H-213/Hong Kong." $325.00.

Courtesy Phyllis Kates.

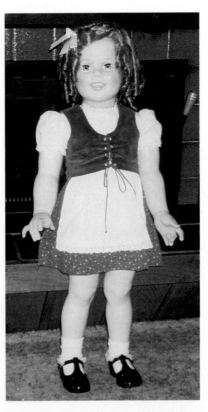

11" REBECCA OF SUNNYBROOK FARM is made of vinyl and has sleep eyes. All original and made in 1983. The six dolls in the set were re-dressed for 1983 and came in 8" to 12" sizes. Others is set were SUZANNA OF THE MOUNTIES, WEE WILLIE WINKLE, POOR LITTLE RICH GIRL, LITTLE MISS MARKER, and DIMPLES. Will be marked 1982. Each - $30.00. *Courtesy Kathy Tvrdik.*

36" SHIRLEY TEMPLE dressed as HEIDI and made in 1960. Shoes and socks have been replaced. There was also a HEIDI in yellow with black bodice and red trim. Uses the PATTI PLAYPAL body. Marked "Ideal Doll/ ST-35-38-2" on head and "Ideal" in oval with "35-5" on body. $1,500.00 up. *Courtesy Theo Lindley.*

8" Japanese painted bisque with painted-on shoes and socks. Doll on left is redressed and marked "S1224/Made in Japan." Doll on right is in old dress. Marked on back "Made in Japan/ S 1223." Each - $285.00. *Courtesy Martha Sweeney.*

Celluloid SHIRLEY TEMPLE dolls. Left: 7" dressed in original glued-on crepe paper clothes. Mark is bell with "K" inside it. Right: 10" is redressed and has painted-on shoes/socks. Bell mark plus "Made in Japan." Paper sticker on right side of head is "Made in Japan/Action Passed ECT M.A. I.N.S." inside circle. 7" - $185.00; 10" - $265.00. *Courtesy Martha Sweeney.*

⇜ Terri Lee ⇝

TALKING TERRI LEE with a soft Swiss fiber wig in a brunette color. All original. Shown with original striped box and "Dolly's Lullabye" record. From 1950. $500.00. *Courtesy Susan Giradot.*

16" TERRI LEE in original trunk and with two tagged dresses. Missing shoes and socks. Doll only - $325.00. *Courtesy Frasher Doll Auctions.*

16" TERRI LEE in original dress, sunglasses, and hat. The shoes and socks have been replaced. $325.00.

Courtesy Frasher Doll Auctions.

16" TERRI LEE in original tagged sundress. $325.00.

Courtesy Frasher Doll Auctions.

16" TERRI LEE in original tagged dress. $325.00. *Courtesy Marie Ernst.*

16" TERRI LEE made of painted hard plastic. Has brunette manniquin wig. All original and tagged. $400.00. *Courtesy Susan Giradot.*

TERRI AND JERRI LEE made of all hard plastic. Both have tagged clothes as doctor and nurse. Original. Each - $400.00. *Courtesy Patricia Wood.*

16" TERRI LEE COWGIRL wearing a satin blouse and felt outfit. Has side part hairdo. $400.00.

16" JERRI LEE with caracul wig. Wearing an auto-graphed Gene Autrey outfit. (Autograph is on left pants pocket.) Outfit was sold separately for both the TERRI LEE and JERRI LEE dolls but was not made to go on the Gene Autrey doll. $400.00. *Courtesy Susan Giradot.*

16" TERRI LEE looks good as an Indian. Clothes are original. Hair pulled to back. Beaded headpiece may be an addition. $400.00.

10" TINY TERRI LEE walker with sleep eyes. Dressed in tulle and net gown with pink and silver lamé formal coat and beaded pearl tiara. All original. $225.00.

Courtesy Susan Giradot.

TINY JERRI AND TERRI LEE in matching card print romper and dress. He has caracul wig and she has saran hair. Both are original. Each - $185.00. *Courtesy Susan Giradot.*

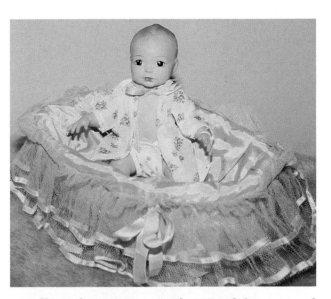

11" all vinyl LINDA BABY with painted features and dressed in tagged outfit. Sitting in original bassinette trimmed with chiffon net and satin ribbon. $200.00.

Courtesy Susan Giradot.

Left: TINY JERRI LEE with auburn wig wearing blue jeans and checkered shirt. Right: TINY TERRI LEE with hard-to-find platinum wig wearing blue striped school dress. Each - $165.00. *Courtesy Susan Giradot.*

TALKING KEVIN doll from the 1991 movie, *Home Alone.* Pull string talker made of all cloth with vinyl head, molded hair, and painted eyes. Made for Twentieth Century Fox and distributed by T-HQ, Inc. $42.00. *Courtesy Jeannie Mauldin.*

11" VANILLA ICE, popular rap star from the 1990s. Has molded flat top hairdo. Distributed by T-HQ, Inc. in 1991. $36.00. *Courtesy Kathy Tvrdik.*

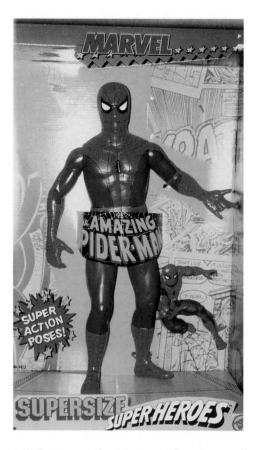
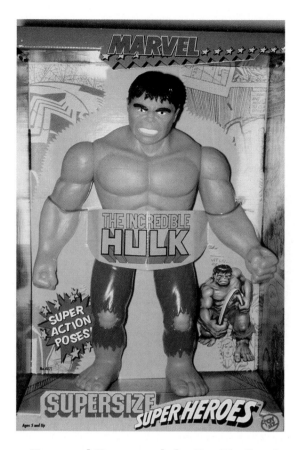

15" SUPERSIZE SUPERHEROES SPIDERMAN, INCREDIBLE HULK, and VENOM made by Toy Biz, Inc. in 1991. Marked "Mfg. by Toy Biz, Inc./1991 Marvel." Each - $30.00–35.00. *Courtesy Don Tvrdik.*

4½" Sergio Valente male with motorcycle. All vinyl with painted hair. Made by Toy Time Inc. in 1982. Licensed by English Town Sportswear Ltd. Set - $35.00. *Courtesy Marie Ernst.*

Black version of Sergio Valente figures. Both are made of vinyl with painted features. He has painted hair; she has rooted hair. Horse belongs to girl and is named Amber. From 1982. Each - $22.00. Horse - $8.00. *Courtesy Marie Ernst.*

Left: 2" Troll made by Russ in 1980s. Right: 4½" Ski Bum Troll made by Dam Things, Inc. in 1986. 2" - $12.00; 4½" - $20.00. *Courtesy Gloria Anderson.*

Left: 3" Lucky Lottery Troll made by Russ. Has brown eyes. Right: 12" Graduate Wishnik Troll with brown eyes and oversized ears. Tagged "Wishnik" by Uneeda. From late 1980s. 3" - $15.00; 12" - $35.00. *Courtesy Gloria Anderson.*

10½" SALLY STARR with printed felt clothes, plastic boots, and stiffened felt hat. Made of all vinyl with sleep eyes and rooted hair styled into ponytail. SALLY STARR was on "Popeye Theatre" from 1950 to 1972. Doll is from 1959 to 1961 and came in several styles and colors of clothes, but all had her name printed on skirt. $85.00 up. *Courtesy Ellyn McCorkell.*

14" CARMEN as played by Rita Hayworth. All original and very rare, especially in mint condition. Made of all composition and looks exactly like a composition MARY HOYER doll. Has adult figure with stapled-on underclothes and glassene sleep eyes. Dressed by Uneeda in 1948. In this condition - $500.00. *Courtesy Jeannie Nespoli.*

22" BABY GLEE with big smile, wide open/closed mouth, molded tongue, and deep dimples. Has vinyl head on cloth body. Thumb and two fingers on left hand touch. Marked "Uneeda Doll Co., Inc." This example is original and in mint condtion. Made in 1978. $35.00. *Courtesy Jeannie Mauldin.*

8" JANIE is a hard plastic walker with vinyl head, rooted hair, and sleep yes. Dressed in late 1950s Brownie uniform with missing beanie. Original and in mint condition. $65.00. *Courtesy Pat Graff.*

16" MISS DEB with grow hair feature. Made by Uneeda for W.T. Grant in 1971. Has sleep eyes and lashes. Exact same doll was marketed as MAGIC MEG. This one is all original and mint in box. $20.00. *Courtesy Pat Graff.*

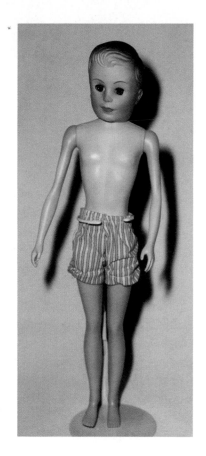

Left: 11" DOLLIKIN made of vinyl and plastic. Multi-jointed and very posable. Marked "Uneeda Doll Co./MCMLXIX (1969)" on head and "Dollikin/US Pat./ 3,010,253/other US & For. Pat. Pend." $35.00.

Right: For over twenty years this lad has needed spinach! This is BOB, the boyfriend to Uneeda's Barbie-type doll, SUZETTE. Has sleep eyes with molded lashes. Marked "Uneeda" on head and body. $20.00.

11" ELLY MAE CLAMPETT (Donna Douglas) from TV's "Beverly Hillbillies" that ran from 1962 to 1971. The doll is marked "Unique" and was used as a premium doll by Kelloggs. Note black buttons on blouse. She was also known as CALICO LASS and wore the yellow dress shown with matching bloomers. $65.00. *Courtesy David Spurgeon.*

Virga

8" Lucy was a Virga doll of the 1950s that was also marketed as Virga Play-Mates. She was a straight leg walker made of all hard plastic with a head that turned. Her legs were slightly curved with a crease in the middle of the knee cap. She had molded-on T-strap shoes that were painted or left natural. Her stomach was quite rounded and had a small dot for navel. The second and third fingers on her hands were molded together. There was a deep indentation under her lower lip but no dimple. Molding seam lines can be seen cut-

ting through the back of the ears. Dolls were unmarked or had "Virga" on head.

Virga was a trademark of Beehler Arts Co. that marketed from 1949 through the 1950s several 8" dolls including Olympic Princess, Joanie Pigtails, Starlet Doll that promoted Lustre-Creme Shampoo (trademark of Inez Hollan House), Ninette, and Kim. Lucy was made as an Indian, Hawaiian, and black. By late 1950, she had a vinyl head on hard plastic body.

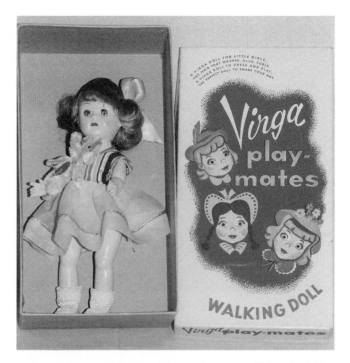

Platinum-haired LUCY as "Majorette." Walker doll with head that turns. Has sleep eyes and molded lashes. This outfit is often passed off as an untagged GINNY. $75.00. *Courtesy Maureen Fukushima.*

8" LUCY shown in original box. She is an all hard plastic walker with head that turns and sleep eyes. Has gray pipe cleaner animal in arms. Poem on box: "A Virga doll for little girls. Has hair that washes, also curls. A Virga doll to dress and play, The perfect doll to share your day." In box - $75.00. *Courtesy Maureen Fukushima.*

Left: 8" LUCY in original box and dressed for "First Communion." Right: Also shown in original box is JOANIE PIGTAILS, the black version of LUCY. Both are walkers with heads that turn from side to side. They have sleep eyes and molded lashes. Each - $75.00. *Courtesy Maureen Fukushima.*

LUCY is ready for the playground. Set has full sunsuit outfit with doll wearing matching panties. Includes glasses, straw hat, and cape to go around neck when hair is washed. Doll is a pin jointed walker with head that turns. In original plaid striped box. $100.00. *Courtesy Maureen Fukushima.*

8" LUCY BALLERINA with pink wig, sleep eyes, and molded lashes. Shown in what is called the "star box." The quality of the doll, clothes, and packaging improved as sales got better between 1949 and 1956. She was still made of all hard plastic until 1958. $75.00. *Courtesy Maureen Fukushima.*

LUCY BALLERINA shown in a window box with theater curtain for background. Made of all hard plastic. Has pink wig and pink tutu. Feet are molded into tip-toe position. Has pearl tiara. $75.00. *Courtesy Maureen Fukushima.*

As seen in the *New York Times* advertisements for Effanbee dolls during 1951, Madame Schiaparelli not only designed clothes for women, but for children, including her our daugher, who was nicknamed "Gosse." That name turned into another nickname by her teenaged classmates – "Go-Go." Virga dolls from 1958 to 1959 came in different style boxes, but all the boxes came in Schiaparelli vivid pink. "Prom" is a LUCY doll with vinyl head, rooted hair, and wrist tag. $100.00. *Courtesy Kris Lundquist.*

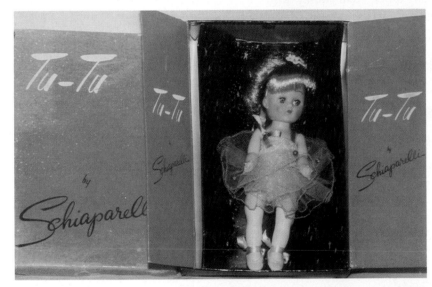

8" TU-TU BALLERINA was designed by Schiaparelli and has rooted blue hair to match her outfit. Wearing leotards and ballet slippers. Note that the feet are molded in tip-toe position. She is a LUCY doll with a vinyl head. $125.00. *Courtesy Maureen Fukushima.*

8" LUCY walker with head that turns. Has complete dress outfit plus jacket, hat, and shoes. She is wearing cape for washing hair. Mint in orignal box that is red, green and blue plaid. $125.00. *Courtesy Maureen Fukushima.*

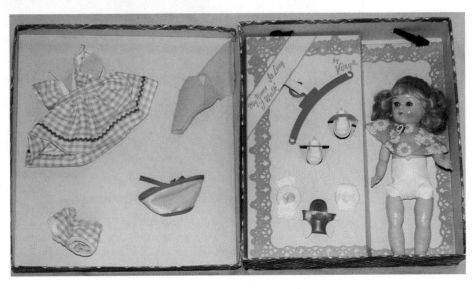

Virga's "Lollipop Series" (green and lavender versions not shown.) 8" dolls in series are walkers. Cosmopolitan's GINGER dolls had different color hair with purple and pink the known colors. Also Nancy Ann's MUFFIES had some with blue and green hair. Each - $90.00. *Courtesy Maureen Fukushima.*

8½" high-heeled teen doll by Virga for Beehler Arts, Ltd. Has joints just above knees and sleep eyes. Clothes are removable, but she looks just like dolls that have their clothes stapled or glued on. $75.00 up. *Courtesy Gloria Anderson.*

ᴄ Vogue ᴄ

7½" TODDLES from 1940s. All composition with painted eyes. All original with gold paper sticker on dress. In mint condition. $450.00 up. *Courtesy Sandy Johnson Barts.*

7½" TODDLES made of all composition with label on bottom of foot that reads "Air Raid Warden." Has gold Vogue paper sticker on leg. From 1940s. All original and in mint condition. $450.00 up. *Courtesy Sandy Johnson Barts.*

CINDERELLA GINNY from the 1952 "Frolicking Fables" series. Also came in a variation with pale blue print gown. $400.00 up. *Courtesy Karen Stephenson.*

8" all hard plastic GINNY with painted eyes. She has never had a wig. Original Vogue outfit, but later than doll. $450.00. *Courtesy Kris Lundquist.*

8" GINNY with painted eyes and glued-on mohair wig. All original and in mint condition. From 1950. $450.00. *Courtesy Susan Giradot.*

GINNY in #168 "Special Debutante Ball" made for Wanamaker's. Had lace tiara with flowers over ears. From 1952. $400.00. *Courtesy Sheila Stephenson.*

GINNY boy and girls dressed as square dancers. Dolls are strung. All have painted lashes. Each - $400.00.

Courtesy Peggy Millhouse.

Left: MARY AND HER LITTLE LAMB from 1952. Right: BO PEEP from 1953. Both are original and in mint condition. Each - $400.00. *Courtesy Karen Stephenson.*

APRIL from the "Tiny Miss Series" of 1952. She is a strung doll with painted lashes. Mint in box. $425.00.

Courtesy Susan Giradot.

One of the dolls from the "Tiny Miss Series" of 1952. This GINNY has a caracul (lamb's wool) wig styled in a poodle cut. The dress also came in blue/white and red/white stripes. Outfit also came on GINNY with regular hairstyle. $400.00 up. *Courtesy Sandy Johnson Barts.*

GINNY with poodle-cut caracul wig. She is from "Valentine Series" of 1952. All original with red "I Love You" heart. In mint condition. $400.00. up. *Courtesy Kris Lundquist.*

Very beautiful strung GINNY with painted lashes. One of the "Tiny Miss Series" from 1951–1953. $450.00.

Courtesy Margaret Mandel.

A group of "Tiny Miss" dolls from 1953. Top row: LUCY, BERYL, and JUNE. Bottom row: GLAD, WANDA, and CHERYL. All are original, except for replaced hat on LUCY, and in mint condition. Each - $425.00 up. *Courtesy Peggy Millhouse.*

TINA from the "Little Miss Series" of 1953. Strung doll with painted lashes. Has center snap shoes. Original and in mint condition. $425.00 up. *Courtesy Peggy Millhouse.*

All original GINNY named JUNE from 1951. Strung doll with painted lashes. In mint condition. $450.00 up. *Courtesy Peggy Millhouse.*

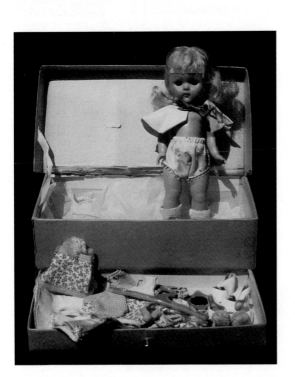

GINNY in 1952 gift set. Cardboard trunk has pull out drawer. It is not known if all the items came with her, but two dresses are missing. As is - $600.00. *Courtesy Kris Lundquist.*

8" GINNY WALKER with molded lashes. Gown is made of taffeta with net overlay and is tagged "Vogue." $350.00. *Courtesy Glorya Woods.*

The first all vinyl Ginny dolls were made by Vogue and will be marked "Ginny" on the head. Lesney of England purchased Vogue Dolls, Inc. and introduced the new Ginny with a thinner body and face. These dolls have sleep eyes. They also introduced the Sasson Ginny with painted eyes in the 1960s. In January of 1973, Lesney sold the Vogue name and molds to Tonka. Tonka eventually sold out to Meritus, who in turn sold the Vogue products to R. Dakin in 1986. Dakin is still producing Ginny dolls and doing a great job of it. Their dolls are more like the original round-faced Ginny dolls of the 1950s.

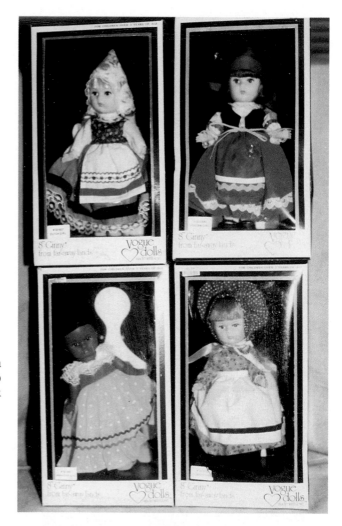

8" all vinyl GINNY dolls with sleep eyes. Made by Vogue in the 1960s. They are dressed in international costumes. Top row: DUTCH and ITALY. Bottom row: JAMAICA and PIONEER GIRL. Each - $50.00. *Courtesy Kris Lundquist.*

Regular GINNY with sleep eyes on left and SASSON GINNY with painted eyes on right. Although the design and manufacturing are excellent, the thinner GINNY did not ring bells with the GINNY collectors who favored the rounder face doll. Each - $50.00. *Courtesy Kris Lundquist.*

Left: 8" GINNY with sleep eyes first came in green/white and blue/white boxes. Center: The new GINNY–FAR AWAY LANDS had a much more colorful box. She has painted eyes. Right: The typical all blue Vogue box holds a thin GINNY with sleep eyes. Each - $50.00. *Courtesy Kris Lundquist.*

The all vinyl thinner GINNY INTERNATIONAL BRIDES had painted eyes. Each - $50.00. *Courtesy Kris Lundquist.*

GINNY returned to being a round-faced little girl when Meritus manufactured the doll. The doll was improved when Meridus sold to R. Dakin, who still has the ownership to date. Each - $30.00.

Courtesy Kris Lundquist.

71-2530 **Ginny On Safari**
Soft vinyl, blue eyes.

71-6090 **Cookie Cutter Ginny**
Soft vinyl, blue eyes.

71-2760 **Flapper**
Hard vinyl, blue eyes.

71-2680 **Corps De Ballet**
Hard vinyl, blue eyes.

71-2720 **Pirate Adventure**
Soft vinyl, blue eyes.

♥71-2730 **Ginny Goes To Rio**
Hard vinyl, blue eyes.

♥71-3560 **Square Dancer**
Hard vinyl, blue eyes.

♥71-6350 **Cat N' Mouse**
Soft vinyl, blue eyes.

71-2550 **Queen of Hearts**
Hard vinyl, blue eyes.

All dolls are vinyl with sleep eyes. From 1990. Each - $30.00 up. *Courtesy R. Dakin advertisement.*

DRESS ME GINNY made by R. Dakin in 1991. She is all vinyl with sleep eyes. The all original outfit is rare and from 1956. The doll was used to display outfit. Doll - $30.00. Outfit - $125.00. *Courtesy Pat Graff.*

Jill was first introduced as Ginny's big sister in 1957. She was a 10½" all hard plastic doll with sleep eyes and high-heeled feet. She had a glued-on saran wig, and her fingernails and lips were red. There was a large variety of outfits available for her.

Jan was another 10½" doll, but she had a vinyl head with sleep eyes and a rigid vinyl body. Her hair was rooted, and she had a slight smile where Jill had a much more serious look. Jan also had high-heeled feet, and she could wear the same clothes as Jill. This was 1958, and as time went on, the Jill head mold replaced the Jan head.

Jeff was introduced as Jill's friend in 1958. He was 11½" tall and had a vinyl head and rigid vinyl body. He is marked "Vogue" on his head.

It should be noted that during 1959 or 1960, some Pink Lip Jans were put on the market. These are attractive dolls and reminds one of the 1960s when the beehive hairdos, heavy Cleopatra-style eye make-up, and no lip color was so popular.

Very mint group of all hard plastic JILL dolls with high-heeled feet and sleep eyes. In the center row is JEFF, who is all vinyl. JILL - each $165.00 up. JEFF - $85.00 up. *Courtesy Peggy Millhouse.*

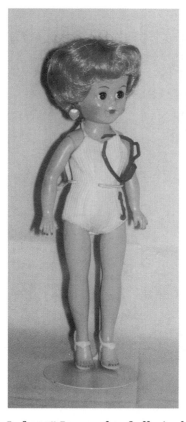

Left: 10" JAN made of all vinyl with slight smile and rooted hair. $165.00 up. Center: JILL is ready for the beach in #3362. $135.00 up. Right: All hard plastic JILL in her lounging outfit #7510. $135.00 up.

Courtesy Maureen Fukushima.

Two beautiful girls in great outfits. GINNY in #3364 and big sister JILL in #3164. This GINNY - $400.00 up. This JILL - $225.00. *Courtesy Maureen Fukushima.*

10½" JILL in outfit #7412 and 8" GINNY in #7512. GINNY has jointed knees and is a walker. This GINNY - $325.00 up. This JILL - $175.00. *Courtesy Maureen Fukushima.*

JILL made of vinyl with pale pink lips. Any of the vinyl JILLS are hard to locate as are vinyl JAN dolls. **$135.00 up.** *Courtesy Maureen Fukushima.*

JILL is dressed for after-five dining in outfit #3382. **$135.00 up.** *Courtesy Maureen Fukushima.*

Left: It is time for a costume party, and JILL **is ready in outfit #3413. $165.00 up. Center: 10½"** JILL **is going for a night on the town in outfit #3460. Note ankle strap shoes. $135.00 up. Right: 10"** JILL **is dressed casual in outfit #3369. $135.00 up.** *Courtesy Maureen Fukushima.*

A very pretty JILL in outfit #7516. These shoes are worth just about as much as the rest of the outfit put together. **$135.00 up.** *Courtesy Maureen Fukushima.*

JILL dressed in outfit #3190, a black evening gown with hot pink hooded cape. **$165.00 up.** *Courtesy Maureen Fukushima.*

10½" JILL in unidentified tagged outfit. She is original and in mint condition. **$135.00 up.** *Courtesy Maureen Fukushima.*

JILL dressed in outfit #3366. She is all original and in mint condition. **$135.00 up.** *Courtesy Maureen Fukushima.*

10½" JILL in unidentified ballgown that is tagged. $185.00 up. *Courtesy Maureen Fukushima.*

This is the JAN doll when Vogue started using the JILL head. Vinyl head with rooted hair. The beautiful ballgown is #3380. $185.00 up. *Courtesy Maureen Fukushima.*

11½" COWBOY JEFF is all vinyl with sleep eyes and molded lashes and hair. $125.00 up. *Courtesy Peggy Millhouse.*

JEFF in his football gear. Original and in mint condition. $125.00 up. *Courtesy Maureen Fukushima.*

17" BABY DEAR designed by Eloise Wilkins who illustrated over 100 Little Golden Books. Cloth body and vinyl head and limbs. Her expression is pouty. Has very small painted eyes. Marked "E. Wilkins 1960" on upper left leg. Cloth tag on back of neck marked "Vogue Dolls, Inc." Made in 1961. $95.00.

17" STAR BRITE made of all vinyl with eyes painted to side and stars for highlights. Made for one year only in 1966. Marked "Vogue Dolls/1966" on head. $50.00.

10½" LIL' IMP is made of hard plastic with vinyl head, rooted orange hair, freckles, and green sleep eyes with molded lashes. Has multi-jointed knees. From 1960. Mint in box - $65.00. Doll only - $45.00. *Courtesy Maureen Fukushima.*

25" BOBBY DEAR ONE and BABY DEAR ONE that represent one-year old children. They have cloth bodies, vinyl heads and limbs, sleep eyes, and hair lashes. Both have open/closed mouthes with painted teeth. Both are redressed. From the 1960s. Each - $185.00. *Courtesy Theo Lindley.*

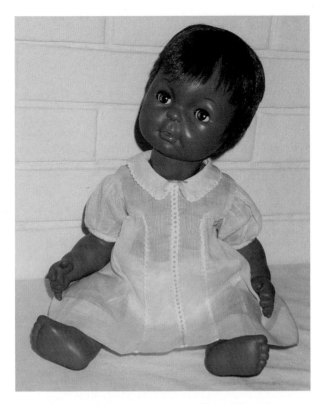

18" black DEAREST ONE that is all vinyl and strung. Very posable head with open nurser mouth. Has been redressed. Marked "Vogue Dolls, Inc./1967" on head and body. $45.00. *Courtesy Pat Graff.*

15" LITTLEST ANGEL with head marked "Vogue. Doll. 1965." Dress is tagged "Vogue Dolls, Inc./Made in U.S.A." Box is marked "Melrose/Tonka Corp." $45.00. *Courtesy Marie Ernst.*

15" MISS GINNY dolls made of plastic and vinyl. Both are all original. Each - $55.00. *Courtesy Marie Ernst.*

17" all vinyl JENNY LIND signed by Robin Woods in 1987. This is a very hard doll to find. $325.00. *Courtesy Pat Graff.*

20" ALEXANDRA is vinyl with cloth body and sleep eyes/lashes. Has a pretty ecru faille dress under coat. Received the 1989 D.O.T.Y. (Doll of The Year) Award. $265.00. *Courtesy Pat Graff.*

14" vinyl SUSAN BLUE made in 1989. $275.00. *Courtesy Pat Graff.*

14" ANNE OF GREEN GABLES is all vinyl with painted eyes. Made in 1988. $325.00. *Courtesy Pat Graff.*

14" SCARLETT SWEETHEART with green painted eyes. All original. This head was designed by Yolanda Bello and is marked "1984" on head. Doll was also used in 1986–1987, then again as FANCY NANCY in 1992. $425.00. *Courtesy Pat Graff.*

14" all vinyl ALISON made in 1990. $225.00. *Courtesy Pat Graff.*

14" ANNA BALLERINA is all original. The flowers in her bouquet are perfection, just as all Robin Woods accessories are. From 1990. $200.00.

⌒ Appendix ⌒

Updated information from previous *Modern Collector's Dolls* series.

• Thanks to Lelani Blessing, we now know about the JOCKEY & HUNTER that appeared in *Modern Collector's Dolls, Series 1,* page 221. These dolls were produced in 1963 by Pressman Toy Corp. (1107 Broadway, New York). In the first year of production, they marketed the JOCKEY, FOX HUNTER, and WESTERN RIDERS. In 1964, they also put out a girl FOX HUNTER. If marked at all, it will be a faint "C" on the back. There was also a line of accessories and horses.

• In *Modern Collector's Dolls, Fifth Series,* on page 268, I thought the two dolls on the lower left were from the movie, *The Black Hole.* I gave the dolls' correct marks of Universal Studios, but *The Black Hole* was a Walt Disney Production. The figures are actually from the television series, "Battlestar Galactica" that was on ABC from 1978 to 1979. The figure on the left is LUCIFER, a Cylon robot. Actor Bobby Short wore the costume, but Lucifer's voice was provided by Jonathan Harris, who played Dr. Smith on "Lost In Space." The figure on the right is BALTAR, played by John Colicos. Lucifer was Baltar's companion.

The two figures on the bottom right of the same page, #268 of *Fifth Series,* are aliens from "Battlestar Galactica" called OVIONS, that were large insect type creatures. The OVIANS were only in the first episode of the series and it is strange that they were made into figures. All are considered hard to find or rare. Thanks to Mary Wernke, a "Battlestar Galactica" fan for the above information.

• Thanks to Terry Richardson, Product Development Manager for Dolls, CBS Toys (Ideal Doll Corp.), for the following information. In *Modern Collector's Dolls, Fifth Series,* on page 171, MY BOTTLE BABY, introduced in 1979, is stated as being called SNUGGLES by 1981. In fact, SNUGGLES was introduced in 1978 as its own entity. There were indeed three different versions of the head but no parts of SNUGGLES or MY BOTTLE BABY were ever interchanged. They were offered simultaneously in 1979 in the same product line. Comments to the previous material: MY BOTTLE BABY is the actual doll shown on page 171 in the *Fifth Series.* It has an open nurser mouth. SNUGGLES did not. Therefore, the bottom line of the caption is incorrect. (There was one version of the SNUGGLES doll that had a mouth that looked nearly the same. The other versions had a slight smile and closed mouth.)

• The following items are from Pat Graff. In the *Sixth Series,* on page 71, Kruger's EVERYTHING NICE and Boots Tyner's GUMDROP are made of vinyl. EVERYTHING NICE is made by Julie Good-Kruger, and it is her 1988 Christmas doll.

• Many people have requested to know who the actors/actresses are depicted by TV series dolls. I have tried to answer all requests in the following list.

"Wonder Woman"
Diane Prince. . . . . Lynda Carter
Steve Trevor, Jr. . . . . Lyle Waggoner
"Lou Grant"
Lou Grant. . . . . Ed Asner
Rossi . . . . Robert Walden
Hume. . . . . Mason Adams
Mrs. Pynchon. . . . . Nancy Marchland
Donovan . . . . Jack Bannon
Animal . . . . Daryl Anderson
"Laverne & Shirley"
Laverne . . . . Penny Marshall
Shirley. . . . . Cindy Williams
Lenny . . . . Michael McKean
Squiggy. . . . . David L. Lander
"Three's Company"
Janet. . . . . Joyce DeWitt
Jack . . . . John Ritter

"Starsky & Hutch"
Starsky . . . . Paul Michael Glaser
Hutch . . . . David Soul
"Kojack"
Kojack . . . . Telly Savalas
"SWAT"
Hondo . . . . Steve Forrest
Hill . . . . Tom Skerritt
"The Waltons"
Mary Ellen . . . . Judy Norton-Taylor
"The Incredible Hulk"
Hulk. . . . . Lou Ferrigno
"Battlestar Galactica"
Starbuck . . . . Dirk Benedict
Apollo . . . . Richard Hatch
Boomer . . . . Herb Jefferson, Jr.
Adama. . . . . Lorne Greene
Boxey . . . . Noah Hathaway
Athena . . . . Maren Jensen
Cassiopea . . . . Laurette Spang
Tigh . . . . Terry Carter
"Charlie's Angels"
Bosley. . . . . David Doyle
Kelly . . . . Jaclyn Smith
Kris. . . . . Cheryl Ladd
"Happy Days"
Richie. . . . . Ron Howard
Fonzie. . . . . Henry Winkler
Howard . . . . Tom Bosley
Potsie . . . . Anson Williams
"Welcome Back Kotter"
Beau. . . . . Stephen Shortridge
Gabe Kotter. . . . . Gabriel Kaplan
Julie . . . . Marcia Strassman
Epstein. . . . . Robert Hegyes
Barbarino. . . . . John Travolta
Washington . . . . Lawerence Hilton-Jacobs
Horshack. . . . . Ron Palillo
Totzie. . . . . Debralee Scott
Verna. . . . . Jean-Vernee Watson
Judy Borden . . . . Helaine Lembeck
Ludlow . . . . Dennis Bowen
Maria . . . . Catarina Cellino
Angie . . . . Melonie Haller
Carvelli. . . . . Charles Flischer
Murray . . . . Bob Harcum
Mary Johnson . . . . Irene Arrange

• There are a lot of exciting artist's dolls that are available and have been for several years. Sales have been high, so much so that they have cut into the regular secondary markets of doll dealers. The artist market has grown to a huge business in a short time.

Many of the doll artists have sold their original molds to mold companies or they have gone into the mold business themselves. Because of this, a monster has been created with reproductions of the sculpted dolls on the market. This can be costly as well as irritating. I got caught in this trap two years ago. While doing appraisals in a doll shop north of Dallas, I looked up all day into a fantastic face that I wanted to take home with me, but I was afraid to ask the price. During the flurry of saying goodbye, getting things together, and leaving the shop, I asked the price. It was $500.00. So I said, "I'll take it." The doll came home and went into a doll case to be admired. When the time came to photograph the doll, I was writing down a description and found only the name of the mold company. The only information I could find out from the shop is whomever made it from an original mold had walked into the shop and sold it to the owner. I'm stuck! I did try to locate the mold company to find out who sculpted the original but could not. This is just one of the complications in original artist dolls, but we can not judge, complain, nor applaud, as it looks as if collectors are buying what they like, and so be it!

It should be noted that over $9,800.00 has been paid for an artist original. Several of the finest artist's dolls around are over $2,000.00. So far, these artists have not sold any of their molds that we know about, and if they sell an entirely different mold, word will spread like the wind, and they will begin to have problems. This pretty well describes what can and does happen in the artist porcelain field and dolls distributed or sold by the artist themselves. Some artists have even made "exclusives" for one of the galleries, mints, or shopping channels and sold those same molds. So one day you may find you purchased a "mint" doll that was made by someone else, like your neighbor or the lady across town.

The vinyl dolls are a different story, yet molds can and have been sold. One must watch the shopping channels, then check all the doll magazines to see what is going on. I have been asked many times to do a book on modern doll artists. Researching this topic became a merry-go-round. I agree a book needs to be done, and soon, before the field gets so confused that it can never be straightened out. So someone out there — take pity on this subject and do the book!

⌒ Index ⌒